Transport without Politics . . . ?
JOHN HIBBS

1. There is a common and rarely questioned assumption that transport is 'special', cannot safely be left to the market, and requires close governmental control of its structure and management.

2. This conventional wisdom has historical roots in the extraordinary emotions aroused by the early railways and the popular belief in the inter-war years that railways should be protected from the upstart road operators.

3. From these beginnings, administrative regulation of public transport has become all-pervasive, imposing territorial carve-ups, cross-subsidisation, quantity licensing, and price controls.

4. Its proliferation has been justified by a variety of defective arguments about economies of scale in the industry, the supposed instability of competition, the requirements of urban land-use planning, the 'co-ordination' problem, and the 'right' of every citizen to mobility.

5. The stifling of market mechanisms has led to misallocations of resources and such large and consistent losses as to create a widespread myth that public transport can never be run profitably.

6. Reform is urgently required to permit the market much wider scope; but little real progress can be made so long as the marginal price of using the costly road infrastructure remains zero.

7. The introduction of marginal pricing related to vehicle size/weight and route congestion would improve efficiency in the use of roads and provide a rational economic basis for re-organising passenger and freight services throughout the transport industry.

8. A national corporation should be given responsibility for the road infrastructure and subsequently for the rail track to facilitate the decentralisation of the railways and marginal pricing of track use.

9. Cross-subsidisation and standard charging in rail and bus should be abandoned; the territorial bus companies should be phased out and their operations transferred to smaller units operating smaller vehicles at higher frequencies.

10. Conurbation transport authorities should be established to co-ordinate land-use and transport policies in the special conditions of major urban areas; they should not own transport undertakings and should have the duty of encouraging de-centralisation in the industry.

Hobart Paper 95 is published (price £2·50) by

THE INSTITUTE OF ECONOMIC AFFAIRS
2 Lord North Street, Westminster
London SW1P 3LB   Telephone: 01-799 3745

IEA PUBLICATIONS

Subscription Service

An annual subscription is the most convenient way to obtain our publications. Every title we produce in all our regular series will be sent to you immediately on publication and without further charge representing a substantial saving.

Subscription rates*

Britain: £15·00 p.a. including postage.

£14·00 p.a. if paid by Banker's Order.

£10·00 p.a. teachers and students who pay *personally*.

Europe and South America: £20 or equivalent.

Other countries: Rates on application. In most countries subscriptions are handled by local agents.

*These rates are *not* available to companies or to institutions.

To: The Treasurer, Institute of Economic Affairs,

2 Lord North Street,

Westminster, London SW1P 3LB.

I should like to subscribe beginning.....................................
I enclose a cheque/postal order for:

☐ £15·00

☐ Please send me a Banker's Order form

☐ Please send me an Invoice

☐ £10·00 [I am a teacher/student at..............................]

Name..

Address...

....

Signed... Date.................

HP95

Transport
without Politics...?

*A study of the scope for competitive markets
in road, rail and air*

JOHN HIBBS

*Director of Transport Studies,
City of Birmingham Polytechnic*

Published by

THE INSTITUTE OF ECONOMIC AFFAIRS

1982

First published in September 1982

© THE INSTITUTE OF ECONOMIC AFFAIRS 1982

ISSN 0073-2818
ISBN 0-255 36155-6

Printed in England by
GORON PRO-PRINT CO LTD
6 Marlborough Road, Churchill Industrial Estate, Lancing, W. Sussex

Text set in 'Monotype' Baskerville

CONTENTS

[3]

[4]

[5]

PREFACE

The *Hobart Papers* are intended to contribute a stream of authoritative, independent and lucid analyses to the understanding and application of economics to private and government activity. The characteristic theme has been the optimum use of scarce resources and the extent to which it can best be achieved in markets within an appropriate framework of law and institutions or, where markets cannot work, in other ways. Since in the real world the alternative to the market is the state, and both are imperfect, the choice between them effectively turns on judgement of the comparative consequences of 'market failure' and 'government failure'.

Transport is a major economic activity which closely affects the lives of everyone in society. Yet it has been strangely neglected by all but a minority of specialist academic economists. John Hibbs, the author of Hobart Paper 95, is one of this small band who has devoted his professional life to subjecting to rigorous market analysis an industry that has fallen into the hands of town planners, architects, engineers, environmentalists, and politicians in national and—especially—local government. It is almost 20 years since the Institute published his first Hobart Paper, *Transport for Passengers*, and 13 years since Hobart Paper 49, *Transport Policy: Co-ordination through Competition*, by the late Gilbert Ponsonby.

Mr Hibbs sets out to challenge the 'conventional wisdom'— which has been allowed to develop partly through the neglect of the economics profession—that transport is somehow 'special' and the allocation of resources and satisfaction of consumer wants in the industry cannot safely be left to market mechanisms.

He traces the origins of this dominant thinking to the emotions and myths of the Railway Age which, when the railways began to experience an erosion of their monopoly position in the inter-war years, inspired widespread popular support for their protection from the competition of upstart road operators. As always, controls bred controls; government interference in the structure and management of transport accumulated at a rising tempo, embracing rail, road and air,

[7]

passengers and freight. Only shipping has escaped. Since the end of World War I, 50 statutes have been concerned with inland transport, two-thirds of them the product of the period since 1945. Irrespective of party, politicians have apparently derived an irresistible fascination from meddling in the industry. The escalation of administrative regulation, purportedly to correct market 'failure', has thoroughly politicised a major sector of commercial activity, grossly misallocating scarce and costly resources—not the least being the distraction of management from its proper function.

Applying the incisive tools of *micro*-economics, Mr Hibbs identifies and analyses the morass of distortion, misallocation and waste produced by 60-odd years of mounting government interference with market forces and normal commercial practice. He exposes the inefficiencies of internal cross-subsidisation and standard charging, lucidly explaining their development as a natural consequence of government-endorsed monopolistic power in the shape of 'territorial' bus companies, quantity licensing, and a railway organisation based on regions rather than systems.

One by one he subjects to critical examination all the standard arguments advanced in favour of administrative regulation: the instability of competition ('fly-by-night' operators and 'competing to kill'); the requirements of urban land-use planning; the inability of the market to co-ordinate and integrate different transport modes; the social problem of the old, the very young, the poor and all without access to the private car; the deprivation of rural communities; and so on. He finds them all weak or wanting, and argues for more market-oriented solutions for problems that are genuine. Most important is his refutation of the widespread belief that monopolistic organisation is inevitable in transport because the industry enjoys very large economies of scale. He contends, on the contrary, that economies cease to apply fairly early in the growth of transport operators and that the optimum size of fleet varies considerably more widely than has been generally thought.

The author is not, however, despairing of public transport. He holds to a firm conviction that it can be made more innovative and profitable, that it can allocate resources and serve consumers more efficiently, if the heavy hand of government control is lifted and much more reliance placed on market forces. Though hesitating to recommend further restructuring of an industry that is already punch-drunk from continual re-organisation, he sees no salvation in the *status quo*. Thus, gritting his teeth, he advances a set of imaginative proposals for reform.

Fundamental to allowing the market to function effectively in transport, he argues, is the introduction of marginal pricing for the use of the road infrastructure, particularly heavily congested urban routes. He suggests a two-part tariff scheme, drawing on ideas put forward in 1964 in the so-called Smeed Report (which G. J. Roth, a member of the Smeed Committee, analysed in IEA Research Monograph 3, *A Self-financing Road System*). An independent, self-financing national corporation —'British Roads'—would take over the ownership and management of the roads from central and local government. It might subsequently also assume ownership and management of the railway track to introduce marginal track pricing and encourage the decentralisation of the railway system.

Decentralisation would become very much the by-word for transport. The territorial bus companies would be phased out and their operations transferred to smaller units running smaller vehicles at higher frequencies. There would be no more cross-subsidisation or standard charging. Administrative control would, however, remain necessary to co-ordinate land-use and transport policies in major urban areas where, because of the scarcity of land and its high opportunity cost, Mr Hibbs doubts that the price mechanism alone would be an appropriate regulator of land use. The boundaries of the administrative bodies established for this purpose would be determined by the requirements of transport and not local government. They would not, however, *own* transport undertakings.

Although the constitution of the Institute requires it to dissociate its Trustees, Directors and Advisers from the author's arguments and conclusions, it presents Mr Hibbs's *Hobart Paper* as an authoritative and incisive analysis of the ills of transport, borne of the author's life-time study of and close familiarity with the industry. His proposals for remedying those ills are imaginative and radical and merit the closest attention of all who have an interest in the efficient transport of goods and people—and that means everyone.

August 1982   MARTIN WASSELL

THE AUTHOR

JOHN HIBBS was born in 1925 in Birmingham, and grew up in Essex. After graduating in the School of Social Studies at the University of Birmingham he entered the transport industry with Premier Travel Ltd. of Cambridge. In 1952 he was awarded the Rees Jeffreys Studentship for two successive years at the London School of Economics, where he obtained his MSc(Econ.) with a thesis entitled 'The effect of the Road Traffic Act 1930 upon the development of the motor bus industry'. In 1956 he managed a bus and coach business in Suffolk before joining British Railways in the headquarters of Eastern Region in 1961, working on traffic survey, costing and market research.

In 1967 he moved to higher education and directed the pioneer undergraduate course in Transport Studies at the City of London Polytechnic. Since 1973 he has been at the City of Birmingham Polytechnic, where he is now Director of Transport Studies. He is also researching for his PhD at Birmingham University on 'A comparative study of the licensing and control of public road passenger transport in selected overseas countries'.

Mr Hibbs's previous Hobart Paper, *Transport for Passengers*, was first published in 1963, with a revised edition in 1971. Widely read both at home and abroad, it played a part in making the deregulation of the bus and coach industry practical politics. His other books include *The History of British Bus Services* (1968); *Transport Studies—An Introduction* (1970); and *The Bus and Coach Industry—Its Economics and Organisation* (1975). Mr Hibbs is a member of Council of the Chartered Institute of Transport.

[10]

ACKNOWLEDGEMENTS

This *Paper* owes much to the late Gilbert Ponsonby, with whom several early drafts were discussed. It has been developed in academic discussion, not least with students, but I have also had the benefit of presenting papers to conferences at which practitioners, planners and politicians have contributed to the controversy. I am particularly grateful to the University of Newcastle upon Tyne for opportunities to present papers to their annual Symposium, and to the Liberal Party's advisory panel on transport. Not everyone who has helped me develop my thoughts will agree with my conclusions. A considerable debt of gratitude is due to Arthur Seldon, Martin Wassell and Michael Solly of the Institute of Economic Affairs, and to an anonymous academic referee, whose comments have led me to sharpen the argument in numerous places. The responsibility for both fact and conclusion remains mine.

J.H.

I. TRANSPORT AND GOVERNMENT

The conventional wisdom

Transport is an activity as basic to human wellbeing as medicine or perhaps even agriculture, yet it is strangely lacking in political or social prestige. It was said of an MP in the 1930s that, when told he was to be made Minister of Transport, he exclaimed: 'Some enemy hath done this!'.

Transport does not rank high as a profession, despite the chartered status of its Institute, whilst as a trade it has no unified lobbying power. It is a large industry, accounting for 5·6 per cent of the workforce on the standard industrial classification, but it is divided by function, mode and ownership. It is hardly surprising that its lobbies are sometimes mutually antagonistic.

Academic study of the industry might be expected to provide one source of a unified approach to the problem of transport. But such study has been late appearing, and until 1939 was largely concerned with railways. The past 10 years have seen the rapid growth of a literature, but there is still much reserve in the attitude of the academic world towards transport studies. We may have to wait a while before the formal study of transport makes a serious contribution to policy, which in the interim will continue to display the confusion and uncertainty that has marked the past 60 years. As a consequence, the conventional wisdom will survive relatively unchallenged.

It is the purpose of this *Hobart Paper* to challenge certain elements of the conventional wisdom in the hope that it may contribute to a more rational and coherent policy for transport. This Section starts by examining some of the components of that wisdom today.

Political intervention in public transport: plus ça change . . .

In 1920, speaking in the debate on the Railways Bill which provided for the 'grouping' into four of the then 120 railway companies, Mr Winston Churchill explained that the Government had considered three policy options: leave the companies

[13]

as they were; nationalise them; or take the middle course he was advocating. In 1930 Parliament passed with a minimum of debate those clauses in the Road Traffic Bill which introduced quantity and price control of bus and coach operation— as had been recommended by a Royal Commission whose chairman, Sir Arthur Griffith-Boscawen, a minor Conservative politician, expected it to promote 'rationalisation as a prelude to nationalisation'. In 1932 Sir James Arthur Salter (later Lord Salter) chaired a conference which recommended quantity control of road goods transport for hire and reward, and whose membership included the railway companies and the few large hauliers but excluded the multitude of small proprietors. And in 1939 a Conservative government effectively nationalised commercial aviation—in the form of Sir John Reith's British Overseas Airways Corporation—after 15 years of rampant subsidy of its 'chosen instrument', Imperial Airways. The notion that the state should intervene in the structure and management of the public transport industry has never been the preserve of one political party; indeed, the nationalisation of railways was first provided for in 'Gladstone's Act' (the Regulation of Railways Act) of 1844.

Nor is it necessary to turn always to the past for examples of government interference with the supply of this essential service. Several recent Prime Ministers have not held aloof from dictating the charging policy of British Rail. And local government affords even more telling examples. Thus, before the local elections of 1981, the Conservative majority on the West Midlands Metropolitan County Council introduced a flat fare of 10p on Mondays for all bus and train services in the county. It was marketed as 'Funday'. Suburban shopkeepers complained bitterly that their trade was being syphoned off, and the monopoly operator reported a net loss of £82,000 per day from revenue foregone and the cost of additional vehicles to cope with demand on some routes in peak periods. After the elections the new Labour majority did away with 'fundays', but subsequently reduced all fares and allowed children to ride anywhere on the system for 2p. The consequent joyriding once again increased peak demand, while regular passengers complained at being unable to rely on getting on a bus. To provide for the planned deficit required the council to issue a supplementary rate demand, but there then followed the celebrated decision of Lord Denning in the case of London

Transport fares, after which the council took advice and restored fares to their original level. (It also gave a rebate on the rates for the next financial year.)

Neither an economist nor a commercially-oriented transport operator would feel happy with policies such as these, which were introduced without market research or analysis of elasticities of demand at varying fares. But the principal issue is the unchallenged assumption that politicians should rightly be expected to take such decisions over the heads of professional managers. For the tradition of government interference in transport is widespread, both in Britain and abroad.

British transport policy, such as it is, may be characterised as protectionist at the national level and interventionist at the local, irrespective of which political party is in power. These attributes are seldom questioned. Politicians and trade union leaders seem to please their supporters or members most by calling for 'integration' or 'co-ordination' or similar ill-defined placebos, while bewailing from time to time the absence of 'a national policy for transport'. (The same people do not complain at the prolonged failure of the EEC to produce a Common Transport Policy, with the implication of free access to the market which the Treaty of Rome would suggest.) Within such a vacuum it is no wonder that public knowledge and opinion are coloured by deeply-felt myths, which have been aptly described as 'fossil emotions'.[1]

The perennial myths

The general acceptance of the assumption that transport cannot safely be left to market forces and is thus a suitable candidate for public intervention can be understood against the background of the long period when the railway companies had a hegemony over all but local movement of goods and passengers, and came to exercise a remarkable hold over people's imaginations. That much opposition to the rationalisation of railways was irrational is now acceptable material for situation comedy. But the degree of emotion which marked the so-called 'Beeching closures' illustrates the depth of feeling transport can evoke. (The closures procedure was blatantly rigged so as to discourage rational and informed debate.)

The network of main railway lines in Britain was completed

---

[1] N. Despicht, *The Transport Policy of the European Communities*, PEP, 1969, p. 83.

by 1870. There were subsequently two developments whose consequences go far to explain the emotions the railways arouse. The first was the extensive construction of branch lines, few of which were ever a sound financial investment. A preoccupation with the need to be connected to the national transport system can be traced back to the days of river improvement even before the Canal Age; and much canal investment had been made primarily in the hope of improved opportunities for trade rather than in the expectation of dividends. The rail branch lines seem to have satisfied a compelling urge to avoid the danger of communities being left to decay through lack of connection to the national network, even though their contribution to local prosperity may in practice have been minimal. The reverberations from the fear of isolation account for the fierce opposition to closure by people who had seldom, if ever, made use of their local line. Yet there was never the same opposition to the withdrawal of *freight* services, which in many cases had been the chief benefit accruing from the original investment.

The second development was the growing belief among traders that the railway companies were abusing their quasi-monopolistic power. This led to the Railway and Canal Traffic Act of 1875. Modern research[1] into the behaviour of the companies as discriminating monopolists suggests that the fears of traders which led Parliament to intervene were more imaginary than real, but its significance as an interference with the commercial freedom of railway managers (as distinct from necessary safety regulation) can hardly be underestimated. It introduced the detailed control over railway charges which continued until 1962, and which was extended in 1930 to the bus and coach industry, where it lasted for 50 years.

Parliament in the 19th century also took a close interest in the structure of the railway industry, resisting mergers until forced to accept their inevitability by the Report of the Departmental Committee on Railway Amalgamation of 1911. The heavy capital outlay required for railway construction severely penalises over-optimistic commercial decisions. For main lines, the point at which no further construction could be justified was demonstrably reached when the London extension

[1] Peter Cain, 'Private Enterprise or Public Utility? Output, Pricing and Investment on English and Welsh Railways, 1870-1914', *Journal of Transport History*, 3rd Series, Vol. 1, No. 1, 1980.

of the Manchester, Sheffield and Lincolnshire company (opened to Marylebone Station in 1899) proved a financial disaster. Here rail contrasts with road transport, where capital intensity is much lower and fixed plant much less important. And mergers are less likely in a free market, where new competition can always keep enterprise on its toes and the penalty for failure is liquidation. Only the most far-sighted recognised that the collapse of the General Strike of 1926 symbolised the end of the Railway Age and the return of competition to the transport industry. The railways had been shown to be no longer essential to the survival of the economy. Yet government and public opinion remained convinced that railways should be protected from the upstart road operators, a view not uncommon in Britain and many other countries to this day.

From the perspective of history, the Railway Age can be seen for what it was—an atypical period in which, for reasons still debated, investment was channelled into a mode of inland transport demanding an unusually heavy commitment to fixed plant.[1] Previously, inland and coastal transport had formed an extended and competitive market, with the ownership of track and terminals separated from the ownership and management of vehicles. It might have been expected that the end of this atypical period would have seen a return to the *status quo ante*, but the change has been resisted, and with considerable fervour. In many countries in continental Europe it has not even proceeded as far as in Britain, which partly accounts for the failure of a common transport policy to emerge in the EEC.

The myth of inevitably loss-making public transport

There is one final, extraordinarily pervasive, myth—that all public transport loses money and must inevitably continue to do so. If this were true there would be no point in the argument of this *Paper*. But it is an unjustified and misleading generalisation. True, most railway administrations are net lossmakers, although there are several notable exceptions in the United States. It is, however, in inquiring *why* they lose money that the second part of the myth is shown to be a *non sequitur*.

[1] T. R. Gourvish, *Railways and the British Economy, 1830-1914*, Macmillan, 1980, pp. 12-19, summarises the differences that still exist among economic historians about the early patterns of investment in railways.

Few railways in the 20th century anywhere in the world have been permitted that element of profit-maximisation that the return of inter-modal[1] competition would have justified. In almost every country they have been subjected to debilitating regulation and statutory control over their prices, which has in turn starved them of capital even where they still had access to the market to raise it. Many have been saddled with expenditure which belongs more logically to welfare or defence budgets. Railway managers (and economists) have acquiesced in this incubus for far too long, clinging to an outdated belief that they still had the duties proper to a monopolist when their monopoly had already disappeared. And, finally, they have reaped the reward of their paternalistic attitude to labour in the legacy of confrontation which makes it so hard for management and trade unions to work together to create the profitable railways that could still come into being. The attitude of railway trade unionists should not be condemned without taking into account the treatment they received at the hands of the companies after the General Strike.

The generalisation that all public transport inevitably loses money is equally unjustified when it comes to urban passenger transport. Many urban authorities throughout the world subsidise their buses, trams and metro services, but as a deliberate policy of discouraging the use of the private car. As will be seen (pp. 56-57), special problems arise from the scarcity of land in urban uses. But what is sometimes called the 'continental approach' (which uses large subsidies to give buses and trains an advantage over the private car) is only one way of dealing with them. In Buenos Aires, for example, which is a European-style city with a population of 10 million, some 80 per cent of public transport passengers travel by bus, and the small companies providing the bus services—with small vehicles operating at a high frequency—are profitable. The cost of congestion caused by the private car is the true problem, and there are ways of overcoming it which do not undermine the working of the market.

It is commonly assumed, though seldom enunciated and even less often challenged, that there is something special about transport—particularly railway and urban transport—

---

[1] 'Inter-modal'—a term in common use in transport to indicate the relationship between modes (e.g. between the bus and the private car), as distinct from the relationship between firms within a mode.

which exempts it from the normal 'laws' of economics and necessitates a much closer control by government than would be expected of any other industry. This assumption will be analysed in Section II. Suffice it here merely to note that the administrative solution is most often preferred to that of the market in tackling transport problems; that such little trust is placed in the ability of the entrepreneur to solve them; and that governments have for long ignored the evidence that no significant economies of scale exist in the industry.

II. ALTERNATIVES FOR POLICY

Allocation and public choice

The conventional wisdom about transport holds that its resources are better allocated by administrative decision than by the market. To what extent is this assumption borne out by the facts?

A great deal of the industry is still firmly in the market sector. More than three-quarters of the goods moved in Britain are carried by road. Road goods transport has some 125,000 firms, with an average fleet size of four; only 100 firms have 200 or more vehicles. They are all subject to quality licensing, including the strict limitation of drivers' hours. The multitude of smaller firms are probably price-takers (many of them sub-contractors of larger neighbours), and rates in general are the product of market forces, though there is guidance from the trade's representative bodies—the Road Haulage Association (for the public hauliers) and the Freight Transport Association (for the own-account[1] fleets).

Passenger transport is more complicated. To begin with, 82 per cent of passenger-miles are by private car. And of the 5,607 bus and coach firms in 1980, 5,504 are in private owner-ship with an average fleet size of five; only 20 have more than 50 vehicles (Table I, p. 41). The traffic, however, is unevenly distributed, with the private sector accounting for only 10 per cent of the passenger-miles by bus and coach. Yet the large statutory operators that dominate public transport are subject to the same quality control as their smaller competitors and, since the 1980 Transport Act, there has been little price control.

Bus and coach operation thus ranges from small firms, mostly engaged in private contract work, which are unequivo-cally in the market sector, through the operating subsidiaries of the two state-owned holding companies, which are under

---

[1] 'Own-account' signifies the use of vehicles by companies for the carriage of their own products. There is no longer any legal distinction between public and own-account haulage, but in practice there is very little overlap.

[20]

a statutory requirement to balance their books, to the municipal undertakings and Passenger Transport Executives with their quasi-monopoly status. All are still subject to the oversight of the regional Traffic Commissioners,[1] whose quantity control remains a significant cause of imperfection in the market served by scheduled services.

Just as there is little pressure to bring the road goods operators and the coach proprietors under administrative control, so also little serious thought is given to returning the larger passenger transport undertakings to the discipline of the market. The privatisation of the state-owned road haulage business—formerly the National Freight Corporation, later the National Freight Company—by selling it to its own staff met with broad political approval, but urban public transport is widely seen to be a proper function of public enterprise and planning—as is the management of the railways.

The strength of this faith is remarkable; even to criticise it is to risk being thought eccentric. It is found throughout the world, not least in the USA where urban transport is commonly regarded as a 'utility'. Significantly, it is also closely linked to the pervasive assumption that urban transport and railways must inevitably be provided at a loss, to a greater or lesser degree. Of most interest here is that the assumption is not a product of political ideology but reflects a widely-felt rejection of the market as a means of making transport provision respond to public choice.

It does not, however, extend to a *complete* rejection of the market. The private car (or lorry) competes with state-owned transport, which is thereby forced to undertake aggressive marketing. In Britain, the state-owned railways pioneered the car-carrying trains now so common throughout Europe and developed the Freightliner concept[2] as a means of retaining merchandise traffic. Furthermore, at the prompting of the National Board for Prices and Incomes in 1968,[3] they success-

---

[1] Their function was analysed in a previous *Hobart Paper* by the present author, No. 23: *Transport for Passengers*, 1st Edn., 1963; 2nd Revsied Edn., 1971.

[2] Freightliner trains run to fixed timetables and carry only standard containers. They enable railways to carry the range of 'merchandise' for which traditional freight trains were never well suited, and they also simplify the transfer of goods from and to the road vehicle at each end of the railway's part of the haul, by avoiding the need to 'break bulk'.

[3] Report No. 72: *Proposed Increases by the British Railways Board in Certain Countrywide Fares and Charges*, Cmnd. 3656, HMSO, 1968.

fully used the freedom of charging given them in 1962 to introduce a discriminatory fares policy which has done much to improve their finances. On the Continent, urban public transport
authorities have paid much attention to improving their
services, both technically in the design of vehicles and even
more through the development of methods of charging and
fare collection that simplify life for the passenger. (Their activities are also an abnegation of any policy for 'fine tuning' the fare
structure to reflect variations in the elasticity of demand.)

These matters are closely related to the central issue of
economies of scale, which will be further discussed (pp. 39-42).
The question here is whether important parts of the transport
industry must necessarily be subject to central administration.
The arguments in favour are plausible and must be countered
before the return of more sections of the industry to the market
sector can be advocated.

Arguments for the status quo

Perhaps the most deeply entrenched argument for administrative control of one kind or another is that which stems from
the supposed instability associated with competition. In the
intellectual and political climate of the inter-war years it expressed itself as a widely-held distrust of atomistic competition
of the kind which characterises unregulated road transport.
It has led in turn to the encouragement of 'combination' in
countries with widely varying political systems. It is true that
examples of outright consolidation in the hands of a single
corporation have been relatively few in the West and in developing economies; and, indeed, decentralisation is still to be
found in countries with centralised economic systems. Yet
quantity control of bus operation is the rule rather than the
exception, and it is usually designed to inhibit the working
of the market.

That this is so may perhaps be explained as a characteristic
response of bureaucracy to atomistic competition. A system
of quantity control, in which entrepreneurs are required to
prove 'need' before entering the market, has a spurious air
of equity, while a procedure whereby the 'established' operator may object on grounds of financial damage to his
business removes the issues from the market-place to the
rarified atmosphere of administrative law. Furthermore, the

[22]

system allows the established operators to act as policemen, thus deflecting criticism from the bureaucrats and relieving them of the necessity for an interventionist stance. Such a system will of course stifle the dynamic of the market, which enables the changing variables of demand and supply to be mixed and matched. But bureaucrats dislike change and place a premium upon stability, which can be justified only if it is in the long-run interest of the consumer.[1]

Is fear of instability a real danger in a market for public transport?

What, then, is this supposed danger of instability? Among professional hauliers, firms come and go, the less efficient failing when trade is depressed and with newcomers always standing ready to enter the market.[2] Traders shop around for the best rates, while operators adjust the scale of their operations to current demand. Despite occasional grumbles, the system seems to work well, with satisfied customers and satisfactory returns on capital. The only experiment with outright nationalisation in the British Isles—that of the Northern Ireland Road Transport Board from 1935—proved a failure and was abandoned. So if the 'instability' said to be inherent in road transport is not an obstacle to the movement of goods, why should it be an obstacle to the movement of people?

The growth of the bus industry was marked by swift and sometimes confusing change, especially in the decade of rapid expansion after 1919. Much of the story has passed into the realms of myth, notably because the larger firms saw it in their interest to discredit competition and so defend the monopoly rights they enjoyed under the Road Traffic Act of 1930. There are few reliable sources to turn to for the historical truth since most records are more or less tainted in this way. But what can be pieced together seems to suggest neither disaster nor Utopia, as indeed might be expected. Change there certainly was as operators came and went during the course of development. Yet there is little firm evidence that passengers were discommoded by it. It is very likely that they stood to benefit from the process, in which operators, large

[1] What is equally significant is the tendency for politicians of all parties to concur in these views.

[2] The Foster Report (*Independent Committee of Inquiry into Road Haulage Operators' Licensing*, HMSO, 1979) did not consider it was the function of statutory regulation to protect business men from the consequences of their own mistakes.

[23]

and small, fought to establish themselves and thus built up a network of services far more quickly than could conceivably have happened under a blanket of state control.

Because of the vested interest of established operators as well as the bureaucrat's distrust of change, it is as important as ever to regard the fear of instability with a critical eye. Two recent developments reinforce this advice. In the first, the state-owned bus companies have been driven by economic circumstances to undertake market analysis programmes (MAPs)[1] which, though limited largely to adjusting supply to existing use, are a belated departure from their traditional attitudes. Why it should take a financial crisis to bring this change about may prompt us to reflect upon the bureaucratic nature of much state enterprise. The state companies have defended their monopoly for many years on the argument that market forces bring instability. But is instability such a high price to pay when set against the innovations market forces encourage?

The second example is the phenomenal growth of long-distance coach traffic after deregulation in 1980, and the exploitation of market segments following the abolition of price control. Why was deregulation so vehemently opposed—on the ground of fear of instability—by those firms (including the National Bus Company) which subsequently benefitted enormously from it at the same time as they were improving services to the public?

In theory, there would seem to be two reasons why an element of instability associated with over-rapid change might follow from a whole-hearted return to the market (as distinct from the cautious measure of deregulation introduced in 1980). The first is the risk that large firms with financial reserves might use their economic power to 'compete to kill'—that they might seek to drive their competitors off the road by rate wars and dangerous practices. This was by no means unknown before regulation was introduced in 1930 when it was very commonly initiated by the larger firm whose traffic was taken away by a smaller competitor.

It may be that the risk is less important now that significant doubts have been cast upon the existence of economies of scale in the industry. If, however, that danger was still thought to exist, it would not be difficult to devise a system of checks

[1] Further discussed below, pp. 70-71.

and balances to contain it. And these could also deal with the second possible source of instability, that of 'fly-by-night' competition, where (probably smaller) operators move onto a route to take a quick profit and depart.[1]

All in all, it is hard to see why a somewhat atavistic fear should be allowed to inhibit the advocacy of the market in transport as the preferable alternative to a stultifying system of administration.

Is central control necessary for optimal resource allocation?

Control is also defended on the ground that it is necessary for the optimal allocation of resources. It is the argument of the central planner. Yet, significantly, managers in the transport industry respond to it in a rather ambivalent way; they accept it as strengthening their hold on monopoly, but resent it when it starts to remove decision-making into the hands of the planners. It is here, in short, that government and transport may conflict.

The argument usually takes two forms, one related to urban land-use planning, the other to the social problems of insufficient demand. A serious and wholly commendable attempt to deal with these issues lay behind one of the memorable White Papers which marked Mrs Barbara Castle's period of office at the Ministry of Transport in the 1960s and which one can only admire even while differing from their conclusions. They led directly to the Transport Act of 1968,[2] which forms the framework of the publicly-owned bus industry of today.

In the 1967 White Paper, *Public Transport and Traffic*,[3] it was recognised that the town planning process, in its land-use aspect, had little instrumental link with the operational aspects of transport. From this conclusion came the idea of 'Conurbation Transport Authorities' (CTAs), with wide co-ordinating powers, to bring the two activities into balance. They subsequently became the Passenger Transport Authorities

---

[1] Proposals for amending the legislation were included in the author's Hobart Paper 23 (1st Edn.), *op. cit*. They would require operators to obtain service licences, to which they must conform for a minimum period (unless prevented by, for example, serious financial loss). No objections would be permitted, and the system would be regarded as an interim measure to be discarded if it proved unnecessary.

[2] Appendix 1, p. 83.

[3] Cmnd. 3481, HMSO, 1967.

(PTAs) of the 1968 Act, with extensive trading rights and the option to exercise a monopoly of public transport operation in their areas if they so wished. The PTAs were required to set up Passenger Transport Executives (PTEs) to carry out their policies, and these bodies were given wide-ranging duties and powers of 'co-ordination' (including compulsory purchase) but little idea of what that over-worked word was supposed to mean.

An integrated transport system?

The argument was, and remains, that the planning of urban bus and rail services should be integrated into the development of the road infrastructure (so-called 'transportation planning', a specialism introduced from the USA in 1960). Until Sir Colin Buchanan pointed out the cost in both investment and disutility,[1] transportation planners had been working on the assumption that they should provide for the forecast expansion in private car ownership. In contrast to much continental European practice, they had not seriously allowed for an improvement in public transport as an alternative strategy, a weakness which can be blamed upon the narrow professionalism of both planners and transport operators. (The education of transportation planners still permits them to qualify without exposure to the problems and processes of *operation*, although since 1980 at least an element of planning is compulsory for the operator's professional examinations. Unfortunately, operators can practice without passing these examinations.)

The PTEs have done something to change urban transport through investment schemes such as the Tyneside Metro and the much more modest cross-city train service in Birmingham. But strategic investment of this kind cannot replace the day-to-day interaction the White Paper expected would solve the urban transport problem. Furthermore, under the 1968 Act the PTEs acquired the transport undertakings of all municipalities within their areas and then directed considerable effort to the organisational consequences of setting up such giant businesses. (Some went further and used their powers also to acquire state and privately-owned transport businesses.)

The Local Government Act of 1972 had a dramatic effect

---

[1] Colin Buchanan, *Traffic in Towns: A study of the long-term problems of traffic in urban areas* (commonly known as the 'Buchanan Report'), HMSO, 1963.

upon the PTEs. The new Metropolitan County Councils it established were to be Passenger Transport Authorities under the 1968 Act, which thereby automatically created two new PTEs and radically altered the boundaries of the existing ones. It did this with no consideration of transport realities, adding Southport to Merseyside, Sunderland to Tyneside, Coventry to the West Midlands, and creating new organisational problems in the forced marriage of former municipal undertakings in such cities as Bradford and Leeds. It also made the PTE a transport committee of the Council, which was against the original idea and seriously diminished the scope for associating planners and operators—a weakness compounded by the planning powers the Act gave to the second-tier authorities. As a consequence, for example, Birmingham City Council has been seeking to construct a bus station which the West Midlands PTE has had to say it would not use (Birmingham City Transport had said the same thing to the planners some years before).

The balanced approach

The first formal statement in the UK of an assumption about urban transport which is common in continental European countries—namely, that public transport subsidies should be seen as part of a 'balanced approach' to the investment problems posed by the private car—was enunciated in 1972 in the *Report of the Expenditure Committee on Urban Transport Planning*.[1] Subsidisation, it argued, is necessary to ensure that public transport is sufficiently attractive to reduce demand for massive road investment that would be destructive of urban form. This superficially appealing argument has become the conventional wisdom in some professional circles. It is usually held to require the final abandonment of those market mechanisms and disciplines over the use of private transport which do exist (even though they are attenuated and of limited effect).

As Section III will show, there is a basic weakness in an urban transport policy which permits road space, a very scarce commodity at certain times and places, to have a zero

[1] HC Paper 57-I, Session 1972-73, HMSO, 1972.

[27]

price at the margin.[1] It distorts the supply and cost aspects of private transport, to the detriment of the public transport operators; and it is compounded by the hidden subsidies enjoyed by private motorists through the absence of an economic basis for parking charges. To attempt to regulate the financial aspects of this situation by a balancing trick that purports to equate revenue support with capital spending has inherent weaknesses and hardly seems to warrant the retention of monopoly power and the inhibition of innovation in urban transport.

If close administrative control and the abandonment of the market are supposed to be a pre-requisite for the rational use of urban land for transport purposes, they are difficult to justify on the experience of British legislation to date. Their real consequence is the politicisation of urban transport, which is a very different thing. The size and complexity of modern cities and their inhabitants' reasonable expectation of a well-ordered society do necessitate some overall strategy commanding respect through the democratic process. It is clearly one option that such a strategy should include the administrative control of passenger transport, making railway and bus services (and, logically, the use of cars) an instrument of the planning authorities. But it is not the only option. Also conceivable is a strategy which imposes a competitive pattern on the provision of public transport—within minimal bounds— and so pursues the benefits to be gained from the market solution.

Social aspects of mobility

The second argument for administrative control turns upon the social aspects of mobility. It really concerns the impoverishment of certain sectors of the population—notably the elderly, women and young people in less affluent areas—for whom public transport does not at present provide an alternative to the private car that is readily available to others. It is commonly claimed that society has a duty to provide an 'adequate' public transport service, funded as may be necessary

[1] This technical economic term is best illustrated by the contrast between electricity supply, where each unit is charged for individually, and water supply, where the amount we use makes no difference to what we pay (except for households which have paid for metering to be installed). As with water, we do not pay for the use of roads on any kind of unit basis and so have almost no incentive to assess the cost and benefit to us of each extra trip.

through transfer payments. This view is seen to demand government ownership and administrative control of the system, supposedly to minimise costs by avoiding the element of profit.

Mr Mayer Hillman and others[1] have drawn attention to the volume of unsatisfied demand for mobility and the hardship that it may represent, although any attempt to present 'access' (to shops, doctors, relatives, and so on) as an absolute good must fail to impress if the same is not claimed for the biological necessities of life. The appeal to a supposed golden age of public transport in the past must allow for the low wages that went with it. Moreover, the marginal cost pricing of electric current for traction enabled tramways to charge very low fares in an age when the base load of a power station was current for lighting. Even so, as a recent study has demonstrated with some rigour,[2] there is comparative deprivation in our cities that would hardly be tolerated if an acceptable method of ending it could be found.

What is remarkable is the size of this unsatisfied market. Pressing the comparison with the market for foodstuffs and other consumer goods, where a range of supermarket chains each caters for a sector (defined largely by socio-economic class) of the total market, it is surely permissible to wonder whether urban passenger transport might offer a satisfactory return to businesses with an equally sharp nose for the price and quality each sector prefers. Why should there not be 'Sainsbury' buses and 'Quicksave' buses, and various other brand names in between, all catering for different market sectors and making a living from it as their supermarket equivalents do?[3] Instead we have the uniformity of the administrative product, on offer at standard prices irrespective of variations in cost of production or elasticity of demand.

It will be objected that urban transport in the USA has

---

[1] Mayer Hillman with Irwin Henderson and Anne Whalley, *Personal Mobility and Transport Policy*, PEP Broadsheet 542, PEP, London, 1973.

[2] Morris Bradley and Stephen Thompson, *Getting There: A survey of teenagers and young women, using cars or living without them in Glasgow*, Scottish Consumer Council, 1981.

[3] This kind of market differentiation has indeed started to be developed in the provision of express coach services since deregulation in 1980. National Express is catering for the mass market at cut fares and with standard vehicles, while, along with some smaller firms, it offers higher standards at higher fares, sometimes including meals, drinks and films *en route*. It remains to be seen how far the process will be taken.

[29]

decayed to such dangerous levels as to have made a large contribution to the social problems of American cities, and that the market cannot be relied upon to satisfy demand at an acceptable price. The reply is that the US operators seldom functioned in a competitive market. Bus operation in the United States has for many years been constrained by licensing similar to that in Britain. And, in practice, the assumption that public transport is a 'utility' (in the American sense of the term)[1] led to most transit businesses acquiring monopoly rights. Whether private or 'public', monopoly seems to yield questionable results in satisfying the market for mobility in towns.

The accepted method of dealing with the problem of unsatisfied demand, in Britain as in many other countries, is by transfer payment. Insofar as this is merely a subvention from public funds to keep fares low, it is an extremely blunt instrument and totally destructive of market mechanisms. (The case for a subvention to raise the quality of service, perhaps above what the market would offer, is discussed as a separate issue.) But even where the subvention is to a sector of the market, such as old-age pensioners' passes bought from the operator and providing free or reduced-cost travel, it reinforces monopoly unless the scheme can be made available to any operator who wishes to enter the market.[2] The alternative of fostering a market system is successful in many cities abroad (p. 61), and it is no exaggeration that prejudice is the main reason why it is not seriously considered for Britain.

The remaining arguments for the administrative solution seem largely to follow from the tacit assumption of its superiority. Thus it is claimed to be necessary in order to permit marketing improvements, such as transfer bookings and methods of pre-payment.

Most of these arguments are very much retrospective, and their net benefit to the public is not often assessed. Pre-booking was not unknown in the era of competition, and firms in competition might be expected to promote it in order to enlarge their market share. Transfer bookings and various

[1] Really 'public utility', as, for example, the telephone system—an industry that is inherently monopolistic and therefore subject to public control.

[2] In Northern Ireland—where there is ironically only one bus operator apart from the state-owned Ulsterbus—old-age pensioners are not given travel passes of the usual kind, but may purchase tickets at a reduced rate on demand; these are then 'redeemed' by the appropriate authority for the balance. Such a technique could easily be used in a competitive market to avoid distortion.

methods of charging by time instead of by distance are not ruled out, even in a market, but might have to be supervised to prevent their being developed as a barrier to new entrants. In any event, it seems likely that a relatively small proportion of journeys requires a change from one public vehicle to another on more than one occasion.

Is administrative control required for 'co-ordination'?

There is also the vague but often persuasive argument that administrative control alone is conducive to the pursuit of the much-praised but ill-defined objective of *co-ordination*, which does not lend itself to rigorous analysis or measurement. Railways originated as point-to-point carriers, but rapidly developed to become the pioneer industrial organisations under pressure to minimise transaction costs when providing a nationwide service to the consumer.[1] But railways are differentiated by their technology, and also tend to benefit from what Professor Williamson calls 'economies of scope'[2] so long as they can exploit a monopolistic position. The same circumstances do not apply in the freight transport industry, with its emphasis on manageable cost centres; to extend them by analogy to bus and coach operation is theoretically unsound.

The organisational structure of the bus industry undoubtedly owes more to the principle of cross-subsidisation, which was the conscious argument for developing the 'territorial' bus companies and the rather less explicit justification for municipal operation. It remains the unspoken argument for the preservation of 'networks'. If it can be shown that the network illustrated in the map at the back of a timetable booklet has objective value to the consumer such as to offset the advantages of the market, then transaction cost might be a relevant principle. So far, however, such a value has been assumed rather than demonstrated. (Merely ensuring that public

---

[1] On the economic significance of this development, O. E. Williamson, 'The Modern Corporation: Origins, Evolution, Attributes', *Journal of Economic Literature*, XIX, 4, December 1981, pp. 1.537-68, especially pp. 1, 551-3.

[2] *Loc. cit.*, p. 1,547 n. Also Kent T. Healy, 'The Merger Movement in Transportation', *American Economic Review*, LII, 2, 1962. Both authors refer to the obvious economies of scale that may follow from a railway that has alternative routes between its main sources and destinations of traffic—i.e. the 'scope' of its operations—and both observe that this is a special and limited case of economies of scale.

[31]

services connect with each other might be left to the co-ordinating mechanism of the market, save that history tends to show operators in a poor light in this respect, falling somewhat short of enlightened self-interest, perhaps because of a certain narrowness of imagination. But since those who possess a territorial monopoly are not above reproach, it cannot be made an argument for the administrative solution.)

Does the passenger-customer require protection when the freight-customer does not?

Before concluding this section, it is important to establish whether there is any reason to suppose that administrative intervention might be justified in passenger transport, when it is not thought necessary in the carriage of goods (except for the maintenance of safety standards). The difference between the two modes turns upon the degree to which purchasing power gives the consumer an effective lever to influence supply—with the complicating factor of 'own-account' transport in, on the one hand, the private car and, on the other, the ancillary transport fleet. The 'own-account' aspect has markedly different consequences in each case.

If the purchasing unit for transport is taken as the 'trip' for passengers and the 'consignment' for freight, a notable contrast exists in the span of decision-making. With the exception of the chartered vehicle, there is one decision-maker for each trip—the passenger; in freight transport, one decision-maker will be responsible for many consignments, usually over an extended period. In freight transport and distribution, therefore, the customer has considerably more 'clout' than the individual passenger. Furthermore, the freight transport industry is divided roughly equally between the public transport sector and the fleet of vehicles owned by firms for the carriage of their own goods. Firms dissatisfied with the service provided by public transport have the alternative of supplying their own. The equivalent of 'own-account' transport for passengers is the private car, which many dissatisfied customers cannot afford or are unable to use for one reason or another.

While we can only estimate the number of people who must depend upon buses or trains for their travel requirements, we can start from the statistic that, in 1979, 42 per cent of households in Great Britain did not have the regular use of a car. We

[32]

can then proceed to the 44 per cent which had the regular use of one car only and observe that, for many (if not most) of them the car would have been used predominantly for commuting by the breadwinner. Even allowing for the 13 per cent of households with two or more cars, there must have been at least 50 per cent of the population—and probably more—for which the car is not a realistic option.[1] Most of them are likely to comprise women, the young, the old, and people of relatively low socio-economic standing. These are people who by definition are the least vocal in expressing their preferences. Despite their considerable potential purchasing power in aggregate, they tend to have little influence upon the standards or amounts of supply.

These circumstances are made worse by the monopolistic and paternalistic attitude of the industry, reinforced by statute, which has prevented the market from matching supply with demand. It is indicative that the 'pirate' operator of urban buses in Cardiff, who attracted no little obloquy from the establishment, started by running late-night 'disco buses' to take young people home to the city's housing estates. But it is not enough to assume that deregulation alone would quickly modify the homogeneous supply that has been typical of bus operation for so long; the ethos of paternalism is strong and respectable, and its replacement by a thrusting, market-oriented approach may require a considerable change of heart among managers. In Cardiff, there was evidence that many small operators resented one of their number challenging the established order of things.

Cross-subsidisation and charging

Considerable weight was attached by the Royal Commission on Transport[2] of 1929-31 to the argument that intervention in transport is necessary to permit internal cross-subsidisation. Since economists in general, and for good reason, regard cross-subsidisation rather as parsons regard sin, the question arises why it has so strong a hold on policies for transport.

Much ink has been spilled on how to charge for public transport. One thing is, however, certain: there is no precise method

---

[1] Assuming that one member of each one-car household will have priority in the use of that car.

[2] *Second Report: The Licensing and Regulation of Public Service Vehicles;* 1929-30, Cmd. 3416, HMSO.

of relating each customer's payment to the individual cost of carrying him or his goods. This difficulty led many economists to announce that railways were subject to so heavy a burden of joint costs that there was no point in seeking to analyse them or allocate them to individual services. It was well known that some lines and traffics lost money (although modern costing would suggest they were not always those thought to do so at the time); and it was widely assumed that the railways —perhaps as a consideration for their monopoly strength— could be expected to 'carry' these losses out of profits made elsewhere.

Such a policy was feasible so long as the railways were not subject to serious competition from other modes, that is, so long as their economic position was protected by their technological superiority. It was also logical to extend it to the street tramways as they began to expand at the end of the 19th century, especially since they had the advantage of marginal cost pricing in the supply of electric power before industry began to provide a day-time load for the generating stations.[1] The consequence was an attitude to pricing which survives today in urban passenger transport, although it is, significantly, absent in the inter-city and road freight branches of the industry.

The commitment to cross-subsidisation which had come to be the basis of transport policy was extended without question to the municipal bus fleets and the territorial companies. The concomitant practice of standard charging—with its apparent equity—became the conscious aim of the Traffic Commissioners appointed under the Road Traffic Act of 1930.[2] But the notion of cross-subsidising over wide areas (which were themselves largely adventitious) originated in the formation of the first territorial company, the East Kent Road Car Co., in 1916. It was then that Walter Wolsey, of Thomas Tilling, and Sidney Garcke, of British Electric Traction, devised the 'area agreement' as a means of avoiding mutual competition between the subsidiaries of their respective holding companies. The

---

[1] It was no accident that both municipal and industrial enterprise frequently built power stations and tramways at the same time. The growth of an industrial load in later years forced traction rates up to average costs and undermined the economic advantage of the tram and the trolleybus.

[2] D. N. Chester, *Public Control of Road Passenger Transport*, Manchester University Press, 1936.

area agreement companies became the units for internal cross-subsidisation, without public consultation or approval. (With amendments, they are the operating subsidiaries of the state-owned bus undertakings of today.)

The philosophy established in 1916 expressed itself in a wealth of emotive phrases such as 'using the fat to fry the lean' and accusing newcomers of intending to 'skim the cream off the traffic' while others were 'bearing the heat and burden of the day' (there was a Gilbertian humour latent in the Traffic Courts when the big battalions were mustered against some innovatory applicant for a road service licence—as there still is today). But the advent of the private car as a mode of mass transport after 1950 put an end to the possibility of extracting super-profits and thus to the possibility of cross-subsidisation as it had been practised for so long.

What is cross-subsidisation?

The definition of cross-subsidisation is clearly critical to this discussion. Fortunately, the late Gilbert Ponsonby's contribution provides help.[1] Cross-subsidisation arises where, over an extended period, a service is provided which fails to earn sufficient revenue to cover its escapable costs—that is, the ones to which Ponsonby refers in his incisive question: 'Would we be better off if we did not run it?'. In such cases the firm must rely upon profit in another part of its business if it is to remain solvent—or, of course, upon direct subvention from government. There is no doubt that, at the end of the 1950s, British Railways would have been better off to have withdrawn many loss-making services on branch and cross-country lines, and that the cross-subsidisation the railways had traditionally practised out of their profits on main-line express services had pushed those fares so high as to enable the express coach, with higher *unit* costs, to undercut them.

On this definition, cross-subsidisation definitely excludes the element of common cost present in all transport activities. It also excludes the ups and downs of trade, and the fact that an operator may find it worth continuing into the off-peak period of the day, week or year—even to the extent that escapable costs may be incurred for a short time—so as to

[1] G. J. Ponsonby, 'What is an Unremunerative Transport Service?', *Journal of the Institute of Transport*, Vol. 30, No. 3, March 1963, pp. 90 ff.

'keep faith with the market' and preserve net revenue over the longer term.[1] It excludes by definition the practice of marginal cost pricing (and the so-called 'back-load problem'[2]). And it allows for the possibility that commercial considerations may discourage over-zealous attempts to discriminate too finely between the incremental costs attributable to different passengers on an individual journey.

The amount of true cross-subsidisation practised in the transport industry will probably never be known. Its significance may be illustrated by two arguments from history. First, if in the 1930s the railways had progressively withdrawn from loss-making lines and concentrated upon the fast inter-city services they are best fitted for, would they not at one and the same time have protected those services from road competition and provided an incentive for the coach operators to develop a useful and viable network of cross-country routes? Secondly, if the territorial and municipal bus undertakings had not sought to extract monopoly profit in certain parts of their systems, would they not have been able more effectively to respond to the competition of the private car in the 1960s?

The inefficiency (and inequity) of standard or 'scientific' charging

As we have seen, cross-subsidisation implies standard charging, and this the industry was forced to accept (with little resistance) by the Traffic Commissioners. The 1950s were notable for the pride with which managers of the larger undertakings spoke of 'scientific pricing'. It simply meant charging the same rate per mile for every customer, regardless of variations—either by time or by place—in cost and, above all, in the elasticity of demand in response to changes in price or quality. The apparent equity of this system is contradicted by the hidden transfer payment when some passengers are made to pay more than they consider the service worth while others

---

[1] G. J. Ponsonby, 'The Problem of the Peak, with Special Reference to Road Passenger Transport', *Economic Journal*, March 1958, pp. 74 ff.

[2] Where a firm has sent a lorry with a load to a distant destination, it will pay it in the short run to find a load to carry in the reverse direction at any price exceeding the additional cost thereby incurred, since the lorry has to come back anyway. A temptation is thus presented to unscrupulous 'clearing houses' to exploit the situation to benefit the shipper in the short run. But the longer-term effect in depressing rates may drive transport firms out of business and eventually permit the survivors to charge more. Whether this matters to interests other than the suppliers who tolerate it is open to debate.

are permitted to pay less (such transfers tend to be regressive). It is also a negation of marketing, inhibiting any attempt to match fares with variable standards of quality and has perhaps done as much as anything else to discourage the maximum use of public transport. (It is, of course, attractive to management since it relieves them of the task of assessing the market.)

In a change of policy stemming largely from the Low Report of 1960,[1] the government freed the railways in 1962 from the necessity of cross-subsidisation by undertaking to make up from taxation any shortfall on individual services managements might wish to withdraw. (The ensuing difficulties about measuring the shortfall need not blind us to the potential advantages of this approach.) Subsequently, and at the suggestion of the National Board for Prices and Incomes,[2] British Railways abandoned standard charging and introduced a discriminatory fares policy that has done much to maintain the revenue of its inter-city network and maximise passenger loads by attracting marginal customers. Only in 1980 did the bus operators receive a similar freedom, which they are now cautiously exploring (though the municipal operators still seem to be wedded to standard charging).

Complexity and obscurantism

Cross-subsidisation is a complex issue which has obscured the discussion of policy for many years. Practised over wide areas, it implies transfer payments which are both unrelated to any feasible welfare calculation and likely to be regressive. It also distorts the allocation of resources, and implies the necessity for state-enforced monopoly. Yet the purist attempt to make each element of transport self-financing, or even to identify suitable services for direct subsidy, comes up against the age-old problem of indivisibility. As Dr James Crowley writes in a penetrating discussion of competition in air transport:

'. . . the normal pattern for airline operation is the definition of a home base and the development of a network labyrinth surrounding the base. How the airline's fleet of aircraft is deployed over the network is usually the subject of a complicated scheduling process with numerous interlinkages, some positioning flights

[1] *Report from the Select Committee on Nationalised Industries upon British Railways*, HC Paper 254—I, HMSO, 1960.

[2] Report No. 72, Cmnd. 3656, *op. cit.*

and the deployment of spares. The essential point is that the costs of the various routes are tightly interwoven and that, except in some highly simple situations, the concept of a non-arbitrary individual route cost is meaningless.'[1]

This description will be familiar to managers in many other modes of transport. (Ironically, it is perhaps least true of urban bus operation where resources are normally allocated to individual routes; yet, paradoxically, this is the one sector where cross-subsidisation and monopoly are most strongly advocated.)

Two conclusions appear to follow. The first is that averaging over such a labyrinth confers a net benefit so long as it does not imply failure to cover escapable costs—an important gloss on Ponsonby's approach to cross-subsidisation which has interesting implications for the structure of the industry (pp. 70-71). The second leads to the questioning of the conventional wisdom which seeks to justify the large fleets that typify the bus industry (but not the coach trade) today. The optimum size of fleet may be much smaller than it is customary to assume.

When the market has been given the fullest possible opportunity to satisfy the demand for transport, there may yet be areas where, through imperfection or (more usually) the geography of settlement, some people are unable to secure reasonable provision. In such cases society, through its elected representatives, may decide to alleviate the relative deprivation of certain of its members.[2] This argument is often put forward against the market solution and in favour of treating public transport as a 'utility', in the North American sense. Yet to do so is to abandon *ab initio* the very benefits of the market that tend towards the optimal satisfaction of demand. The time-honoured alternative of cross-subsidisation, as has been seen, has perverse effects. Part of the case for a market solution lies in its ability to *minimise* the cost of any subvention and to indicate objectively the point at which it should be applied.

The techniques of subvention deserve the closest scrutiny since it is not beyond the wit of market operators to maximise

---

[1] James A. Crowley, 'Competition in Air Transport', *Journal of Irish Business and Administrative Research*, Vol. 3, No. 1, 1981.

[2] This must, of course, imply 'taking transport to the passengers'; an 'efficiency maximising' policy would imply moving all the houses, schools, hospitals and so on to the main roads! To some extent we have to live with the locations that people choose.

their earnings from this source. It may well be that the most cost-effective technique is to 'buy' an increase in quality (for example, higher frequency) rather than set out artificially to lower fares.

The issue of scale

For many years it has been widely believed that economies of scale in transport are so large as to lead inevitably to combination and the emergence of monopoly control over wide territorial areas. If this were so, it would have to be admitted that the market solution was inapplicable and that the problem of allocation was best left to administrative decision, with state ownership as the fiduciary alternative to the retention of monopoly profit in private hands.

Yet, to begin with, this belief is plainly contradicted by the structure of the road freight transport industry (see p. 20). It has been seen that road passenger transport showed a tendency to territorial organisation as early as 1916, which the licensing system underwrote after its introduction in 1931. It led to the emergence of the 'territorial' bus companies which were finally brought into state ownership between 1949 and 1968 and which, after 'rationalisation', have become today's subsidiaries of the National Bus Company and the Scottish Bus Group. Licensing also established the monopolies of the municipal transport departments, usually within local government boundaries but in some cases as territorial operators in their own right. The municipal undertakings varied considerably in fleet size, while the holding companies of the pre-nationalisation era[1] had seldom sought to re-arrange their subsidiaries to fit any preconceived notion of optimal scale.

It is impossible to know whether the large territorial companies which came to dominate the bus industry after 1931 would have had the same strength without the protection of licensing. It is significant, however, that the representatives of the combine pressed strongly for its introduction in their evidence to the Royal Commission.[2] A feasible hypothesis might predict a state of tolerable equilibrium between 'large' and 'small' operators, in the absence of barriers to entry to the market; but it would be subject to many provisos. What

[1] British Electric Traction, Thomas Tilling, Red & White United, Scottish Motor Traction, and the small Balfour, Beattie group.

[2] Royal Commission on Transport, 1929-31, *Minutes of Evidence*, HMSO, 1931.

appears to be clear, and contradicts the underlying assumptions of the 1968 Transport Act and the re-organisation which followed it, is that the optimum size of fleet varies considerably more than has been generally thought.

The issue of scale has received much attention from academic economists. Those who have examined the transport industry broadly agree that economies of scale cease to apply fairly early in the growth of the firm, and this contention appears to be borne out by the absence of very large firms in the unregulated sector.

Measuring scale is not altogether easy; the fleet size which is optimal for one geographical area, or one type of operation, may be sub-optimal for another. Little work has been done to establish the appropriate parameters.[1] Most laymen would probably reflect upon the remoteness of management in the larger undertakings, whether state- or municipally-owned; and this aspect also emerges in the size of the 'administrative tail' which increases broadly with the size of fleet[2] (Table I). Perhaps the most interesting measure, first suggested by Mr A. F. R. Carling in 1951 and now attracting renewed attention, is the size of the workforce, which should not be so great that the general manager knows nothing of the majority of his staff.

There seems good reason to doubt the argument that size improves efficiency—and railway operation is no exception. The tendency to merger in some aspects of transport was examined by Professor Kent Healy in 1962, before the US railways ran into economic difficulties. He concluded that the possibilities of economies of scale are as limited in railways as in other modes of transport.[3] There exist, as he points out, economies of *density* which arise from carrying more traffic over

---

[1] Considerable variations are found in operating circumstances (e.g. density of population, mean distance of urban settlements, nature of rural settlement, etc.), quite apart from the type of operation (e.g. stage, express, contract, etc.). There are also regional differences in propensity to travel.

[2] The wide divergence in the number of staff per vehicle between public and private sector firms can no longer be accounted for by the employment of conductors, who have become an endangered species. It probably represents to some extent the use of part-time drivers by firms with marked seasonal peaks but reflects chiefly the fact that small businesses have small overheads. (Their overheads would tend to be bigger if they were more extensively engaged in the provision of line services with a larger annual mileage.)

[3] Kent T. Healy, 'The Merger Movement in Transportation', *American Economic Review*, Vol. LII, No. 2, 1962.

TABLE I

BUS OPERATIONS IN BRITAIN, 1980:
STAFF EMPLOYED PER VEHICLE OWNED

Type of operator	Average staff per vehicle	No. of fleet operators	Average fleet size
London Transport Executive[1]	5·49	1	6,185
Passenger Transport Executives	4·36	7	1,479
Other municipal operators	3·38	51	111
National Bus Company subsidiaries	3·61	37	432
Scottish Bus Group subsidiaries	2·96	7	519
All public-sector operators	3·99	103	406
Private operators	1·25	5,504	5
All operators	2·91	5,607	12

[1] Buses only.

Source: Transport Statistics Great Britain, 1970-1980, HMSO, 1982.

a given system, but they simply reflect the very low short-run marginal cost that is characteristic of railway operation because of the lumpishness of investment. True economies of scale from enlarging the whole system are another matter; Healy's researches suggested to him that: 'In the case of the very largest firms, the diseconomies more than offset economies of density'. He quotes as a parallel Mr Stephen Wheatcroft's remark about European airlines that

> 'economies which follow from large-scale operations begin, after the medium scale of operations is reached and the major economies have been achieved, to be offset by the diseconomies of scale'.[1]

For the purpose of this *Paper* it seems reasonable to conclude that the conventional assumption of 'bigger is better' requires careful and critical analysis. Its theoretical foundations are, to say the least, questionable. The examples of the unregulated coach operators and of the road freight industry, in so far as

[1] Stephen Wheatcroft, *The Economics of European Air Transport,* Manchester University Press, 1956.

[41]

they are comparable, suggest there is in practice no single optimum size of fleet in road transport, but that the average fleet size in the public sector bus industry is very much larger than an unfettered market would produce. The issue goes beyond the classic theory of economies of scale (although the literature[1] questions their existence); it turns also upon the extent to which these large organisations can respond to changing conditions, and how sensitive they can ever be to market indicators. Their history over the past 30 years suggests they perform inadequately on both counts.

This Section opened with the question: Do the facts support the assumption that the administrative solution is preferable to that of the market? The answer must surely be: They do not.

---

[1] Among a variety of authorities are: J. Johnston, 'Scale, Costs and Profitability in Road Passenger Transport', *Journal of Industrial Economics,* Vol. IV, 1955-56; M. E. Beesley and Janet Politi, 'A Study of the Profits of Bus Companies, 1960-1966', *Economica,* New Series Vol. XXXVI, 1969; and N. Lee and L. Steedman, 'Economies of Scale in Bus Transport: Some British Municipal Results', *Journal of Transport Economics and Policy,* Vol. IV, 1970.

III. THE CONSEQUENCES FOR ORGANISATION

The impulse to meddle

Irrespective of party, politicians cannot, it seems, resist the temptation to re-organise the transport industry. Nineteenth-century parliaments were less inclined to it (although ready to interfere with the freedom of railway managers to set prices); until 1913 they were more concerned to prevent what were seen as undesirable mergers, conferring territorial monopoly. According to the late Mr Rees Jeffreys, it was during the Versailles Peace Conference that Sir Eric Geddes took counsel with Lloyd George to produce a plan for a 'Ministry of Ways and Communications'. The Ministry of Transport Bill which Geddes introduced into the House of Commons in 1919 (how much easier it is today for a government to set up a new ministry!) was intended as a nationalising measure to make transport an arm of government, along with electricity generation, posts and telecommunications. In the Second Reading debate, Geddes told the House of the Government's decision that, in addition to the elimination of competition and the restriction of freedom of enterprise and private management, unified control was necessary. This scheme would have been something quite different from the 'arms-length relationship' subsequently bequeathed to us by Herbert Morrison; indeed, the Commons disliked it enough to delete all the powers of acquisition.

Whatever Parliament may have intended in 1919, government intervention in the affairs of transport operators commenced very shortly after the new Ministry had been established—and has continued at an increasing tempo ever since. Appendix 1 (pp. 82-4) summarises the principal statutes governing inland transport by rail and road. The period has also been marked by a parallel series of statutes for air transport—despite Churchill's original statement that airlines would have to 'fly by themselves'. Only shipping has escaped (which perhaps says something for the political power of the shipping magnates). Well over 50 statutes have been concerned with inland transport since 1919, two-thirds in the post-Second World War period.

The impact of all this upon the industry has been to distract management from its main function, as managers and workers have had to come to terms with each new dispensation. The 'grouping' of railway companies in 1923, accompanied by a revision of the rates schedules (not completed until 1927), diverted management attention from the growth of road transport and inhibited a full-scale review of the competitive position of the railways until it was too late. Since 1945 the railways have suffered three major re-organisations, not to mention various internal restructurings. As Mr Gerard Fiennes has trenchantly observed: 'When you re-organise you bleed'.[1]

The record of the bus industry may appear less drastic, but the protection conferred by the Road Traffic Act of 1930 proved a false shelter from the growth of competition from the car after 1950 and inhibited an effective marketing response. The territorial companies were involved in more or less important reorganisations in 1942, 1949, 1962 and 1968. And the municipal undertakings in the great provincial conurbations, having been left in peace for many decades, had no sooner been absorbed into Passenger Transport Executives under the Transport Act of 1968 than they were subjected to a sea-change under the Local Government Act of 1972. Much of the freedom of action of their managers was removed, bringing them under the direct control of the political majority on the county council. Even the road haulage industry has been nationalised, partly denationalised, deregulated and then reprivatised—all within a period of 35 years.

Political vacillation and intervention

Air transport has been the subject of re-organisation throughout its history, as governments have vacillated between a desire for viable airlines and a dislike of competition. After the failure of the pioneers to pay their way, in the face of subsidies paid by the French and Belgian governments to competing airlines, Imperial Airways was created by the British Government in 1924 as the 'chosen instrument' for state support, with an eye to the imperial lines of communication. Its neglect of internal and continental traffic led to the growth of private

---

[1] G. F. Fiennes, *I Tried to Run a Railway,* Ian Allan, Shepperton, Middlesex, 1967.

airlines in the 1930s, some managed by bus operators whose entrepreneurial skills were inhibited by the new bus licensing system. In 1929, following their policy of cross-subsidisation out of the profits of competing modes, the four main-line railway companies acquired powers to set up joint operating companies to provide air services. A bitter battle ensued from 1933 to 1938, when they applied a 'booking ban' prohibiting railway booking agents from holding an agency for an independent airline. Government stepped in again in 1935 to recognise British Airways as its second 'chosen instrument' and to allocate spheres of influence. Finally, in 1939 commercial aviation was nationalised in the shape of Sir John Reith's British Overseas Airways Corporation.

The industry was again re-organised after 1945 with the creation of three state airlines, one of which, British South American Airways, did not long survive. But the remaining independent companies proved essential, both in their contribution to the Berlin airlift during the 'cold war' episode and in their ability to innovate. After a series of compromises, a system of route licensing for internal services—based upon the bus licensing system—was introduced in 1960. Government intervention has not, however, ceased, largely because any sizeable undertaking must participate to some extent in the international market which is dominated by bilateral agreements between governments and by the cartel-like International Air Transport Association. The two British state airlines were merged in 1972 as British Airways, against the recommendation of the Edwardes Report of 1969.[1] It has recently been felt by some that the merger was a serious error, and a further reconstruction is currently taking place —the latest in a long series of government interventions whose perennial failure to establish a viable industry gives point to the concern expressed in this *Paper*.

Minimal reform for economic efficiency and demand satisfaction

Against this background of recurring upheaval, further reform should be advocated only with hesitation. There are, nevertheless, reasons to suppose that the present organisation of public transport is far from conducive either to the optimisation

---

[1] *British Air Transport in the Seventies: Report of the Committee of Inquiry into Civil Air Transport* (Chairman: Professor Sir Ronald Edwardes), Cmnd. 4018, HMSO, 1969.

of resource allocation or to the satisfaction of potential demand from people who would be willing to pay for transport at a price they found satisfactory. With these objectives in view, therefore, ways in which the industry might be restructured to give it a reasonable chance to pursue its own salvation with a minimum of interference from government w.ll now be examined.

INTER-CITY TRANSPORT

(a) *Air transport: the limitations of geography*

Within the relatively small geographical area of Britain, the value of air transport with its present-day technology is limited by the distance of airports from residential areas and central business districts, and the consequent cost in money and time of each journey. This limitation gives the surface modes, and especially the railway, an advantage over air services on most inter-city routes. It goes a long way to explain the absence of a British internal airline industry with anything approaching mass appeal.

Independent airlines do, however, survive, and it is difficult to see any pragmatic benefit in the existence of a state-owned monopoly carrier. It does not seem that there are scale benefits to be gained, and the optimum size of airline fleet may be considerably lower than conventional wisdom would have it. Yet Dr James Crowley's analysis (pp. 37-8) suggests it is undesirable to attempt too narrow a definition of the unit of output. Airlines will have to compete with surface modes and thus can be left to set their own fares. It would seem hard to justify any regulation of quantity of output beyond what is necessary to prevent the sort of undesirable activity—'competing to kill' and 'fly-by-night' operations—that can be a problem in road transport (pp. 24-5).

We should perhaps look forward to a situation in which locally-based airlines provide a network of routes which include the cross-country links ill-served by rail and road. But setting up such networks requires some 'main-line' operations, and the total market in Britain is small compared with many other countries. The solution may well lie further afield. The EEC, which in principle seeks to promote competition in transport, might take appropriate action to become a common market for commercial aviation in which the independent

[46]

airlines would cease to be specifically British or any other nationality. Combined with a substantial change of policy on airport development, such a step could radically alter the state of the airline industry to the benefit of all.

(b) *Surface passenger transport*

But a more extensive internal airline industry would be unlikely to have a major impact upon surface modes of transport in the market for inter-city services, given the present state of technology. To a considerable degree the long-running rivalry between rail and road has ceased to present the problem it once did; train, coach and car now share the market, each with apparent commercial success. But the degree of competition in that market is clearly limited by the dominance of a few major firms in the public transport mode and by the lack of rationality in the method of charging for the road infrastructure.

Charging for the road infrastructure

The problem of the road infrastructure bedevils all forms of road transport and its relationship with the railways. It is difficult to pursue a policy of deregulation so long as the marginal cost of using the transport infrastructure (except for railways) remains zero. This obstacle was recognised by Lloyd George when he set up the Road Board in 1909 to administer a Road Improvement Fund financed by the new petrol tax. As Rees Jeffreys observed,[1] three powerful political forces op-oposed any such arrangement from the beginning:

(i) the landed interest, fearing it would lose the benefit it could expect from the growth of road transport in a consequent increase in land values;

(ii) the railway interest, fearing the competition of road transport;

(iii) the Treasury, with its traditional dislike of hypothecated revenue.

The third of these forces has had the most lasting and effective influence.

The story of the Road Board and its consequences is a warning to all who seek the rationalisation of infrastructure pricing.

[1] Rees Jeffreys, *The King's Highway*, Batchworth, 1949.

[47]

Lloyd George's 1909 Budget introduced a two-part levy on road transport: a car tax based on horse-power and a tax (initially 3d. per gallon) on petrol. The levy was intended for the improvement of the road system and to transfer the cost of the roads from the rates to road users. The money thus raised was placed in a Road Improvement Fund administered by the Road Board under the chairmanship of Sir George Gibb, previously General Manager of the North Eastern Railway. The Board used some of the funds as grants to local authorities to extend the tarmacadaming of roads. But no relief was provided for the rates.

The Road Board was absorbed by the new Ministry of Transport in 1919, and the Roads Act of 1920 set up a Road Fund to take over the Road Improvement Fund. The intention of the Act was to use the motor taxation flowing into the Fund to shift much of the cost of highways onto road users; but in the event little was done, and the Fund's balances simply expanded. The attitude of the Treasury was finally made plain in Churchill's 1926 budget speech, when the whole principle of linking road taxation to road use was repudiated. Instead, Churchill 'raided the Road Fund' to increase the revenue of the Government—as did his successors until, in 1936, Neville Chamberlain diverted motor taxation directly to the Exchequer. The Road Fund then became a convention in the Civil Estimates to express the sums voted for roads. It was finally wound up in 1955. The cynicism with which the original reform was undermined over the years would be hard to match, but the economist must also criticise the complete lack of debate about the principles of charging for scarce resources, and the total failure of successive governments to appreciate the problems that would follow from their purblindness.

'Freedom of the highway'—legacy of political machinations

Out of this disreputable saga has grown a political and popular belief in the 'freedom of the highway' and the consequent distortion of market mechanisms which underlies many of the problems in transport today. It constitutes the central issue in the relationship between government and transport, and reform is certainly overdue. Road users of all kinds pay substantial sums in taxation, but have little idea of what they are getting in return. And the equally substantial social costs they

[48]

impose are not brought home to them. Only the fuel tax provides a link between cost and price, but since it is seen both by government and by road users as a purely sumptuary tax[1] (and resented as such), it has little micro-effect on the choice of modes of transport.

The issue of infrastructure is at its most acute in urban transport, but its significance for the market for inter-city services must not be neglected. As long ago as 1965 the Allais Report[2] recommended to the EEC Commission that it should be tackled. The policy recommended consists of making the road user pay a combination of two charges: one based upon the known costs his vehicle imposes on the system, the other (reflecting a 'quasi-rent')[3] related to the degree of congestion on each section of route—ranging from nothing to a sum sufficient to deter the marginal user, or to encourage him to transfer to an under-used route (which might well be a parallel railway line). The attraction of the policy is that it introduces a fiscal relationship between the demand of the user for a transport infrastructure and the costs involved in maintaining and developing that infrastructure. By so doing, it brings home to the user the cost of the scarce resources he consumes.

Devolution with competition for the railways?

It is against this background that the organisation of the different modes of inter-city surface transport must be examined, first for passenger travel and then for freight transport. The proportions of passenger movement by each mode are shown in Table II. To a large extent the competition is inter-modal since public transport is dominated by three state-owned corporations: British Rail, the National Bus Company and the Scottish Bus Group. Furthermore, there seems to be considerable market segmentation with many passengers tending to remain loyal to one or other mode—not least to the private car.

The long years of railway history are still seen by most people, and certainly by most railwaymen, as having culminated in 1947 in the unification of the railways under a national

---

[1] A sumptuary tax is one levied explicitly on a commodity or service the demand for which is relatively inelastic, in order to raise net revenue.

[2] *Options for Transport Tariff Policy*, HMSO, 1965.

[3] A quasi-rent typically arises where a system is not in long-run equilibrium, and in this case would be taxed away.

TABLE II
LONG-DISTANCE JOURNEYS: PROPORTIONS
BY MAIN MODE OF TRANSPORT, 1979-80

(Journeys of more than 25 miles other than to and from work)

Mode	%
Train	14
Ordinary or express bus	2
Coach excursion or tour	2
Privately hired bus or coach	3
Car or van – as driver	52
Car or van – as passenger	26
Motor cycle or moped	1
Aircraft	neg.
Other	neg.
	100

neg.=negligible (less than 0.5%).

Source: Transport Statistics Great Britain, 1970-1980, HMSO, 1982.

administration. As Dr Michael Bonavia has demonstrated,[1] this outcome was not by any means inevitable. His alternative scenario, premised on a Conservative victory in the 1945 General Election, suggests the development of multi-modal transport corporations based on the four main-line companies of the inter-war years. Such a solution was indeed sought in the somewhat different circumstances of the Irish Republic where it has not been an unmixed success, while its equivalent in Ulster has been dismantled. Similar developments in Britain proved unattainable since the British Transport Commission was throughout its life so pre-occupied with the problems of its railways as to be incapable of attempting a multi-modal policy.[2]

The then Conservative Government's White Paper of 1952 envisaged devolution to area boards. But the boards succumbed in due course to a centralising tendency seemingly endemic

[1] Michael R. Bonavia, *The Four Great Railways,* David & Charles, Newton Abbot, 1980, pp. 203-4.

[2] Michael R. Bonavia, *British Rail: The First 25 Years,* David & Charles, Newton Abbot, 1981, is essential reading on this subject.

in railway administration. In any event, the philosophy of railway management in Britain ever since nationalisation has been to divide the network for operational purposes into *regions* rather than *systems*. The regional division was chosen largely because it avoided the danger that individual systems might compete with each other—a state of affairs railwaymen could not readily contemplate since, as has been seen, unification was their highest goal.

Simply to state that unification may not be the ideal structure for railways in Britain is insufficient; because the idea is so new and radical, it requires further support. The idea of small networks in air transport has already been discussed (pp. 46-7), and it seems feasible to consider a similar pattern for the railways. Some degree of competition might provide incentives for better performance and even improve the attractiveness of the railways *vis-à-vis* road transport. Furthermore, the 'smaller railways' which would emerge might be more manageable and offer greater job satisfaction to those responsible for them.

There is a common assumption—indeed, it is almost an article of faith—that railways are by their nature indivisible. It is an irony of history that the multitude of companies existing before 1923 should have become a single administration by 1949, whilst over the same period the case for unification was being weakened by the growth of road transport. Before they were grouped together, the railways successfully shared track and terminal facilities in an age when a *national* railway system was far more logical than it is today. Now that the railways have become a series of more or less discrete traffic flows, with the disappearance of the wagon-load traffic which, so to speak, floated around the system, and with road transport providing a far more efficient means of 'serving all sites', the case for smaller railways deserves serious consideration. If smaller railways were combined with the transfer of their infrastructure to a national track authority (discussed on pp. 68-9), the only remaining problem in returning the railways to the discipline of the market would be their perennial deficit.

The deficit dates from 1956 when the business first failed to cover its working expenses. Despite their technical bankruptcy, the railways were maintained by successive governments on a 'deficit financing' basis, which the more professional railway managers resented. Dr Richard Beeching's appoint-

TABLE III

BRITISH RAIL'S FINANCES, 1969 TO 1980

£ million

	Income from railway operations	Government grant for passenger services	Expenditure on railway operations	Net operating profit/loss	Net income from other sources	Overall profit/loss
1969	462·6	61·1	491·7	41·1	7·5	48·6
1970	509·8	61·7	532·0	39·5	8·0	47·4
1971	532·1	63·1	578·0	17·2	9·0	26·2
1972*	564·2	68·2	625·1	7·3	10·5	17·8
1973	581·1	91·4	688·6	−14·5	10·4	−4·1
1974	621·5	154·3	882·9	−107·0	10·1	−96·9
1975**	774·2	324·1	1,150·9	−52·7	10·3	−42·3
1976	924·6	319·1	1,255·7	−12·0	12·1	0·1
1977	1,066·9	336·5	1,399·6	30·9	13·9	44·8
1978	1,223·6	434·1	1,634·6	23·1	14·7	37·8
1979	1,383·1	522·5	1,888·9	16·7	17·5	34·2
1980	1,564·5	633·6	2,250·1	−52·0	23·4	−28·7

Notes: * Income for 1972 included £26·7 million under the Transport (Grants) Act, 1972.

** Expenditure from 1975 onwards includes certain items previously charged to capital account (£64·11 million in 1974).

Source: Transport Statistics Great Britain, 1969-1979, HMSO, 1981, and 1970-1980, HMSO, 1982.

ment as chairman in 1961 heralded an attempt (already begun in some regions) to cut out unremunerative operations. It succeeded in achieving a shaky near-solvency on current account. The post-Beeching finances of British Rail are summarised in Table III. The main conclusion to be drawn must be the continuing inability of the railways to generate funds for additional investment, and even for the replacement of their assets. (There can be little doubt that over-manning is a major cause of this weakness.)

Although there was an earnest attempt in the 1960s to place railway investment and disinvestment on a rational basis, the chronic failure of British Rail to generate a positive cash flow—let alone to develop unaided the technological potential of rail transport—compels it to depend permanently on government for its economic survival.

The philosophy of the Low Report,[1] endorsed by the White Paper on Railway Policy of 1967, gave birth to the notion of the 'social railway' dependent upon subvention from public funds, the scale and application of which are inevitably political.[2] In any event, the Railways Act of 1974 substituted a global subvention for the previous system under which each line proposed for closure was evaluated and subsidised on its own welfare balance.

Despite every attempt to achieve a rational economic base for British Rail, the state remains its paymaster. However, Richard Pryke and John Dodgson suggested[3] in 1975 that a return to positive cash flow was within the realms of possibility (subsequent criticism of their analysis tended to be *parti pris*). The objective of a number of financially-autonomous railway businesses certainly ought not to be dismissed out of hand. And the analogy with railway centralisation and subvention in other countries should not be pressed in view of their very different historical circumstances.

Recent revival of competition in road transport

There has been a return to competition in road transport since the Transport Act of 1980, though more in principle

[1] HC Paper 254-I, 1960, *op. cit.*

[2] The Central Wales line from Craven Arms to Llanelli, for example, passes through marginal constituencies contested by four parties and may thus be immune from objective cost-benefit analysis.

[3] R. W. S. Pryke and J. S. Dodgson, *The Rail Problem*, Martin Robertson, London, 1975.

[53]

than in practice. Coach services with a minimum stage distance of 30 miles (measured in a straight line) can now be operated by any business with the necessary operator's licence. Since deregulation came into effect in October 1980, there has been only limited competition; the state-owned National Travel[1] network has, in practice, been strengthened. This unexpected (and no doubt unintended) development can be explained by the existence of the chain of booking agencies which feeds traffic to the National Travel services. The consortium set up to challenge the state operator was seen as a parallel to the Trailways franchising network[2] which co-exists with the Greyhound Corporation in North America. But it failed to establish an adequate agency structure, and effectively collapsed when the two largest firms involved withdrew in search of higher rewards elsewhere. (It may be significant that Greyhound and Trailways share a highly regulated market.)

Several relatively large operators have refrained from taking advantage of deregulation, no doubt preferring to maintain the *status quo*. After all, the Act deprived them of monopoly rights that were of considerable capital value, and the revenue from their services would be at risk were they to provoke a larger competitor into an aggressive posture. But a number of smaller undertakings (including some in the municipal sector) have entered the trade—with varying degrees of success. Although fingers have been burnt, several useful services seem to have become established. Perhaps the most interesting development has been the encouragement of market segmentation by the abolition of price controls.[3]

Mere privatisation would be unlikely to develop the potential of the industry. Already the standard vehicle is less luxurious than those in South American countries; and the standard of terminal and ancillary services is appallingly low. (Anyone who complains about conditions in British airports should sample the average coach station.) Certainly a network of inter-connecting services has been built up, with nodal points such as Birmingham, where coaches arrive from all directions

---

[1] The trade name of the National Bus Company.

[2] *Trailways* consists of an operating company which also invites other firms to integrate their services with its own (and each other's), retaining financial independence but using a common livery and trade-name.

[3] Note 3, p. 29.

at specified times, thus enabling passengers to make extensive cross-country journeys (British Rail follows the same practice). Those who argue that competition would place this practice at risk should recall that it originated at Cheltenham in 1927, before the coach licensing system was introduced. While it is clearly of value to many passengers, preserving it should not be allowed to stand in the way of a truly innovative and market-oriented express coach industry.

(c) *Own-account transport—the private car*

So far, only the *public transport* aspects of the market have been considered. There remains the *own-account* sector—the private car. It is by no means a homogeneous mode of transport, ranging from once-a-year holiday motorists who cause heavy congestion on the motorways each summer to high-mileage trade representatives using fleet cars. Problems also arise from the concentration of bookings for holiday accommodation on Saturdays, which makes for 'peaking' as in all forms of passenger transport; and from the provision of company cars as fringe benefits, which may draw traffic away from public transport.

The convenience of the private car for door-to-door journeys with no change of mode *en route*—especially where the travellers include children or old people—is such as frequently to offset the cost advantage rail or coach may offer. Even so, with the introduction of an intrinsically more competitive structure for public transport, the potential scope for winning back traffic from the private car should not be under-estimated.

(d) *Competition in freight: can rail freight survive?*

It is noteworthy what little criticism there is of the inter-city freight industry, which functions in a fully competitive market. While there may well be potential for the expansion of the Freightliner service (the permanently-coupled trains carrying containers on regular schedules which British Rail invented), the advent of a post-industrial economy foreshadows basic difficulties for railway freight services. The devolution proposed for the railways in this *Paper* could considerably ease their task in coping with an uncertain future. There may also be advantage in the operation of trains for the 'piggy-back' carriage of road vehicles over certain sectors of track where

[55]

the investment required for improving clearances and providing terminal facilities could be justified by the savings it permitted in road operators' costs.

Road goods transport has its difficulties in a period of prolonged depression and the re-structuring of industry, and it has at times shown a tendency towards rate-cutting which neglects the ever-increasing cost of more sophisticated rolling stock. Nevertheless, its flexibility is enabling it to weather the storm. The small operating units make it easier to respond to market changes through appropriate adjustments to the size of fleets; and the problems of peak demand are mitigated by the practice of inter-hiring,[1] which is also followed by the coaching trade. Of particular interest is the highly competitve market for parcels traffic, which the road carriers (and the Post Office) have developed in recent years at the expense of the railways. Here a small number of firms offer a nationwide service, which is supplemented by the numerous local networks. The relative stability of the system provokes speculation as to whether something similar might be viable for deregulated passenger transport.

URBAN TRANSPORT

Land scarcity and congestion

The problems of transport in our large cities have been so acute for many years that it is doubtful whether an ideal solution exists. The reason for this intractability is the inevitable scarcity of urban land. A city is a concentration of people intended to promote trade, culture and all that is subsumed in the German word for transport: 'verkehr' ('intercourse'). The result is such a degree of competition for the scarce land that the market alone cannot bring about an acceptable allocation. The opportunity costs of public buildings and parks are so high as to render them almost unimaginable in the absence of government intervention and subsidy.

Subsidy is also said to be inevitable in urban public transport—a contention which is, to say the least, doubtful. Since, however, it has gone unquestioned, it has become established as dogma in some influential quarters and has consequently inhibited objective analysis. After all, that the use of subsidy

---

[1] Inter-hiring is the practice whereby operators sub-contract work at what are for them peak periods to others for whom the peaks occur at different times.

is widespread in Europe and North America does not in itself prove that subsidy is inevitable. The possibility cannot be excluded that policy is mistaken in all countries and that more efficient alternatives are available.

First, there seems little doubt that public transport in our largest cities has suffered from local government re-organisation. It was not necessary for the Passenger Transport Authorities (PTAs) which emerged from the 1967 White Paper, *Public Transport and Traffic*,[1] either to own or to operate public transport. This merely created over-large organisations in the mistaken assumption that they could benefit from economies of scale. (The special case of London Transport was made even worse by failing to provide a co-ordinating body for British Rail as well as London Transport.) The re-organisation of the PTAs under the Local Government Act of 1972 was a by-product of political gerrymandering that contained no transport or planning logic, and merely worsened the new situation.

A comparison of the deficiencies of the PTAs and their operating Executives with the success of some of the smaller municipal transport departments, such as Newport and Reading, reveals the ability of these operators to provide a high standard of quality.[2] Without any commitment to a particular form of decentralisation at this stage, it is possible to contemplate the return of urban public transport to smaller units, together with the retention of a supervisory authority which, relieved of operational duties, would be better equipped to develop and introduce policies to co-ordinate transport with land-use planning and to reconcile the competing claims of public transport and the private car. (These smaller units might include locally-based railway management of the kind already considered: pp. 50-51.)

Is subsidy regressive?

Such a reform would also make it easier to tackle the issue of subsidy. Blanket reductions in fares over an area the size of a British conurbation are as irrational as the blanket increases with which the industry responded to rising costs during the 30 years from 1950. Analysis is urgently required to

[1] Cmnd. 3481, 1967, *op. cit.*

[2] Martin Higginson, *On the Buses: Municipal Bus Operation Under Contrasting Policies*, Polytechnic of Central London, Discussion Paper No. 9, 1980. The other undertakings studied are Southampton, Northampton and Nottingham.

ascertain how far blanket subsidy is regressive in its effect. Certainly it benefits many who do not need such help and penalises many others who cannot or do not take advantage of it. There is reason to believe that smaller units would of their nature use resources more efficiently. Their management might, however, require encouragement to develop creative pricing—as British Rail required the 'nudge' of the Prices and Incomes Board in 1968. With the growth of marketing skills among urban transport managers, the desirability of specific intervention to cater for residual social 'needs'—as in re-housing schemes and the like—would be far more easily assessed.

Deficit financing, whether planned or accidental, is the enemy of efficiency and undermines any attempt to co-ordinate transport and land-use policy. Even more enervating, however, is the unthinking acceptance of standard charging as an equitable means of setting fares.

Some options for policy

1. Smaller units, innovatory management and wholehearted deregulation

An initial option for policy, therefore, is a return to smaller operating units, within such overall control as the scarcity of urban land may necessitate. The value of examples of unrestrained competition cited from disparate conurbations overseas should be treated with reserve in view of the heavy concentration of car ownership within all social classes in Britain. Urban transport policy has to seek to satisfy a broad constituency, otherwise it may become socially divisive. In practice, a wide range of alternatives is available. What must be avoided is a degree of protection higher than is necessary to overcome the problem of scarcity. What must be sought is innovation that passes the benefits of new technology and managerial initiative on to the public as quickly as possible.[1]

The very limited deregulation of urban bus services in 1980 has so far had predictably little impact. But it has succeeded in raising some of the issues underlying the present ownership and organisation of public passenger transport. In Cardiff a local operator obtained licences to compete with the corporation buses on two routes, and started a service that

[1] G. J. Ponsonby, *Transport Policy: Co-ordination through Competition*, Hobart Paper 49, IEA, 1969.

was of higher quality—with improved driving skills and conductors—at lower fares. The customers, while appreciating these advantages, did not apparently value them enough to let a corporation bus pass by and wait for a 'pirate'. For whatever reason, the newcomer ran into cash flow difficulties and eventually ceased to trade.

The Council had meanwhile countered by reducing fares over all its operations and claiming 'unfair' competition (a claim which was reciprocated). Corporation officials—and indeed many private coach operators in the city—seemed to feel there was something improper about the competition; there were confrontations between road transport staff leading to at least one prosecution.

The episode should not be seen as an excuse for writing off competition, which was by no means unhealthy, but rather as an example of the problems that arise when an elected authority has to face a conflict between its interests as a trader and its wider duties to the electorate.

A similar example is suggested by the experience of another newcomer, a firm based to the west of Nottingham which (after a particularly bitter case before the Traffic Commissioners) obtained a licence for a single route connecting a number of suburban centres. Here the Council, which had objected along with the local National Bus subsidiary, met the competition in time-honoured entrepreneurial fashion: it placed one bus in front of and one bus behind the newcomer on his very first trip. This response seems to fit uneasily with the political complexion of the Council, as well as raising the same question as in the Cardiff example about where the best interests of its citizens lie.

These examples, and a handful of others based on similar applications, illustrate the problems that follow from partial deregulation. The Commissioners are now obliged by law to grant a route licence unless an objector can show it would be against the public interest. At the same time, the right to object has been widened to allow virtually anyone a hearing, including recently the Transport and General Workers' Union. The procedure seems guaranteed to discourage any but the boldest innovator. Against a background of reported inertia among smaller private firms, it erects a barrier of litigation which can only add to his expenses. The experience of such grudging deregulation, however, offers no ground to doubt the potential benefits of a more thorough-going reform.

2. *High-frequency urban bus services*

Although to say so challenges the conventional wisdom, the scope for innovation to reduce subsidy and improve quality is particularly large in design—and more especially in the matter of bus size. From the early days of urban transport there has been a consistent trend towards larger vehicles which, for most of the period, has been accompanied by economies of scale and lower prices. The tram-horse could haul a bigger load along smooth rails than the bus-horse could on uneven streets, and the electric tram could carry far more. Early motor buses were small but rapidly increased in size. The trend continued until eventually it gave us the massive double-deckers of today. For most of the period, it coincided with an expanding market.

The last 15 years have seen the size of urban buses grow still larger, while at the same time the market has steadily contracted. What seems not to have been noticed is the link between the two. Passenger transport is a little unusual in that the quantity on offer is also an aspect of its quality—frequency. People do not like waiting for buses and tend to over-estimate the amount of time they spend doing so. If that disutility is minimised by high frequency, they will be more inclined to travel by bus. The industry, however, has called for ever larger buses from the manufacturers in order to maximise manpower productivity. Unfortunately, doubling the size of a bus—other things being equal—requires halving the frequency of the service in order to realise the full potential gain in productivity per driver. It thereby also lowers the *quality* of the service and drives away customers. A downward spiral has been initiated of fewer buses leading to fewer passengers leading to fewer buses.

A second option for policy, therefore, is to reverse this trend, and run buses much more frequently. High frequency is an advantage claimed for various automated systems, with lower labour costs than bus operation. But the investment of capital on such a scale is not necessary; and nor is the disastrously heavy negative cash flow it implies over the period until full network cover is achieved. Existing technology is quite adequate.

Successful urban operators already recognise the requirement of high frequency. Urban bus services in Buenos Aires and Santiago de Chile are operated at one-minute intervals, with bus stops 300 yards apart—and no queues. (They are also profitable, which may be due in part to their operation by small businesses in competition.) In addition to such empirical support for the high-frequency option, Mr J. O. Jansson has recently argued in a notable paper[1] that not only could urban buses operate without subsidy, given a return to high frequency, but also that the improved service would permit fare increases sufficient to generate a positive cash flow.

The one obstacle facing an operator who chose this option would be to find a suitable vehicle. The fashion for large, expensive and complex double-deck buses which has dominated British urban operation for so long has meant that the smaller buses now on the market are built for light loads and low mileage. Nevertheless, the buses that serve the 10 million inhabitants of Buenos Aires are small and sturdy,[2] and the British motor industry must surely be capable of matching them.

3. *Deregulation of urban taxis*

These options by no means exhaust the possibilities for new departures in British transport policy. While the 'jitneys' that are an important part of the scene in many Asian cities may seem too exotic to introduce to our streets (an assumption open to question), there is no doubt that we make very poor use of the urban taxi. The reason is that most local authorities apply a licensing system designed to protect local operators, with the predictable result that, outside London, taxis are high-priced and unreliable. (In London—and, increasingly, other parts of the UK—the uniquely specialised British cab is costly to buy and operate compared with taxis in cities everywhere else in the world.) It is urgently necessary to de-regulate the taxi trade (while tightening up on quality control) to enable it to take its place in the range of urban transport facilities. At the same time, we might also consider the advantages of the 'fixed-route taxis'—found, for example, in

---

[1] J. O. Jansson, 'Optimal Service Frequency and Bus Size', *Journal of Transport Economics & Policy*, Vol. XIV, No. 1, 1980.

[2] They are built locally by Mercedes Benz.

Santiago de Chile—which supplement the profitable bus operations of that city.

4. *Road-use pricing*

The alternatives for urban transport may, therefore, be more promising than is generally assumed. But they will not be sufficient in a country with such widespread car ownership as Britain so long as the infrastructure problem remains unsolved. The Smeed Committee's report on road pricing[1] has been gathering dust since 1964—far too long for the health of our cities. That the price of using the infrastructure is zero at the margin cannot make sense with something so scarce as urban road (and rail) space.

The movement of industrial and consumer goods (some essential to life), the clearance of refuse, the maintenance of road surfaces—all these transport requirements have to share the limited space available with the private car and public transport. The consequence is a degree of congestion that is wasteful because it has no underlying economic rationale. It also creates pollution and frustration. The opportunity for each mode of transport to function at optimum efficiency and benefit to the urban community cannot exist under the present system of road taxation, which is devoid of allocatory logic.

The desirable reform of the system also offers a chance to introduce a method of charging for parking (including the use of private off-street car parks) which would bring home to the user the cost of yet another facility with a hidden subsidy from which he benefits today.

INTER-URBAN AND RURAL TRANSPORT

'An extensive and efficient system'

The British Isles have long been noted for an extensive and efficient system of transport in the countryside. Before the days

---

[1] *Road Pricing: The Economic and Technical Possibilities* (Chairman: the late Professor Reuben Smeed), HMSO, 1964. The report concluded that a system of road-use pricing was both desirable and technically feasible. It recommended a technique using cables buried in the road at intervals which by an induction current would cause a device in the car to discharge a unit as it passed over them. The device would be easily recharged with a cartridge bought from, say, a Post Office, and a light would indicate when it was fully discharged. (G. J. Roth, *A Self-financing Road System*, Research Monograph No. 3, IEA, 1966, pp. 48-51, gives a summary of the various metering techniques considered in the Smeed Report. It is reprinted in Appendix 2, pp. 85-88.)

of the motor bus, the network of railways, now largely dismantled, was supplemented by a local system of omnibuses and carriers. But the entrepreneurs of bus operation rapidly saw the potential of a national bus network. Before private car ownership became widespread, the bus companies had been consolidated into a series of investment trusts with competition between their subsidiaries regulated by territorial agreements. After 1930 this structure was effectively given the force of law and the consolidation of ownership continued.

Today, these companies have come into the ownership of the state through the National Bus Company (NBC), in England and Wales, and the Scottish Bus Group. But the competition from the private car, which began in earnest after 1950, has undermined the cross-subsidisation at the heart of the territorial carve-up; and the 1970s have seen the development of subsidisation from public funds, administered by local government. At the same time, there has been a considerable shrinkage in the number of vehicle-miles in rural areas. The total route mileage, on the other hand, has shrunk less—for a number of reasons.

To begin with, the NBC has withdrawn from a good deal of 'deep rural' operation, partly as a matter of policy and partly in carrying out the threats it makes when faced with a loss of subsidy. Many of its services have, however, been transferred to independent firms. Under the Local Government Act of 1972 the so-called 'shire' counties were given powers and duties to co-ordinate transport services, and they are the channel for applying public funds to maintain unremunerative services. Their policies have varied quite considerably, some being more generous than others. But the fatalistic assumption that rural public transport cannot survive without subsidy is unwarranted. (The examples of rural services which do not require a subsidy deserve further study.) There is reason to believe that a purely market-based solution might leave a significant residue of genuine hardship, but several problems must be resolved before a rational policy can be developed.

The enigma of rural transport—are subsidies essential?

Why is it that, of apparently similar rural areas, some require a subsidy and others not? Although there is always some element of hit-and-miss in the standard of service a village

[63]

receives (such as whether it lies on a main road between two towns), the answer may assist in the formulation of an objective criterion for assessing hardship and justifying subsidy. The present lack of such a yardstick is the biggest barrier to a rational policy for rural transport, as the history of railway closures has demonstrated. It is not a difficulty that will be resolved quickly, although, as Dr David Banister shows,[1] considerable research is being done. It is also in practice complicated by the 'labyrinth' problem already discussed in relation to air transport (pp. 37-8), which inhibits the straightforward identification of costs in a subsidy programme.

Here, as with urban transport, there are advantages in having smaller operating units, as the National Bus Company itself has realised. Marketing skills are also urgently required since, for those who can afford it, the private car is by far the best adapted form of passenger transport for areas of low population. Experience to date with the 'experimental areas' established under the Transport Act of 1980 does not suggest that there is a large reservoir of new initiative waiting to invade the public transport business when quantity controls are removed. The responsibility for encouraging change thus seems to be left with the shire counties, whose co-ordinating officers are already achieving considerable unsung success. The social problem will not go away; the countryside contains a high proportion of people with incomes insufficient to make full use of the private car, whether because they earn less than city dwellers or because they are retired on fixed pensions.

The remaining options for rural transport are limited. The task—which cannot be easy—is one of achieving a successful mix of marketing initiative and such subsidy as may be 'socially justified'. There would be a real danger of pauperising the countryside if state funds were made available to throw at the problem, for country people do not like to feel they are in receipt of charity. But a comparable risk of creating rural ghettoes would follow from relying solely on market forces. It is, however, very doubtful whether quantity control of the kind still maintained over most of the country is in any way relevant.

What must be emphasised is the fundamental difference

---

[1] David Banister, *Transport Mobility and Deprivation in Inter-Urban Areas*, Saxon House (Gower Publishing, Farnborough, Hants.), 1980.

[64]

between urban and rural transport, which may escape many people in a country like Britain where 75 per cent of the population live in urban areas and have little understanding of the transport requirements of rural life.

IV. OPTIONS FOR TRANSPORT POLICY

The central problem

Any discussion of inland transport eventually arrives at the issue of track costs. For many years the consequence was an arid debate whether rail or road transport was unfairly treated —rail because road transport got its track 'free', or road because it paid massive sums in taxation. The debate was necessarily arid because no-one knew what the relationship was between road costs and different classes of traffic. Now, however, much more data is available, and it seems that most road users do pay more in tax than they impose in direct costs—with the exception of the heaviest four-axle lorries (in Britain about 125,000 in number). Whilst it casts some light on the problem of infrastructure costs, this information is of little help in tackling the real economic issue of the method of pricing.

It has been seen (pp. 48-9) that the present system produces a zero marginal price for road use, and consequently has little impact upon choice of transport mode while positively encouraging the inefficient use of scarce road space. The system comprises a sort of two-part tariff, with two fixed elements (the car tax and the vehicle licence) and one variable element (the fuel tax). Demand for motoring is markedly inelastic, and motorists generally perceive their costs to be lower than they are. Thus car users (who dominate the market) are somewhat unresponsive to the variable element, while government regards motor fuel (except for public passenger transport) as a suitable candidate for sumptuary taxation. Car users in turn recognise this as a fact of life and are thus still more discouraged from equating their expenditures with the benefits they obtain from the roads.

In addition, the system inhibits a rational choice of transport modes. The bus passenger perceives that his daily journey would be faster by car and makes his arrangements accordingly. He is then followed by others, until the resulting congestion makes his journey more time-consuming than it had been by bus. By now, however, the bus takes even longer. But, in the

[66]

meantime, the incremental change that has culminated in this absurd situation cannot be reversed unless a sufficient number of motorists return to the bus *en bloc*. It is a sort of prisoner's dilemma. The roads are seen as an amorphous public asset, which everyone owns and to which everyone has an un-qualified right of use, rather than as a resource which the road user should pay for on a unit cost basis. How can transport be successfully returned to the market if the infrastructure—land in alternative uses—continues to be priced in this absurd and wasteful fashion?

It has also been seen (pp. 47-8) how the attempt to carry through this basic reform in 1909 was frustrated, largely if not entirely by the opposition of the Treasury to hypothecated revenue. No politician in recent years has seen fit to question the Treasury wisdom in transport, and the report of the late Professor Reuben Smeed has been ignored. It is claimed that the voting public would not accept road-use pricing and that the transport lobby would oppose it. If such are important reasons for government involvement in transport, little hope remains for a more rational framework for the industry!

Pricing the use of scarce road space

It is not impossible to envisage a corporation—called, perhaps, 'British Roads'[1]—which would own the road transport infra-structure and manage its finances. Its two-part tariff would consist of a licence fee, similar to that now in force, related to the physical costs imposed on the road system by each class of vehicle, and some form of road-use pricing, related to the varying demands for road space in different places and at different times. The methods used could take the form of tolls or supplementary licences to authorise admission to congested areas—although there are drawbacks with each of these systems. (Tolls are probably the most repugnant to public opinion, conditioned as it has been by the idea of the 'freedom of the roads', and supplementary licences have a built-in inflexibility.) An electronic system of unit charging, such as the Smeed Report[2] envisaged, would seem the most effective

[1] The name once suggested by Lord Marsh, who as Mr Richard Marsh was (Labour) Minister of Transport from 1968 to 1969, and Chairman of the British Railways Board, 1971-76.

[2] *Road Pricing: The Economic and Technical Possibilities, op. cit.* (also above, note 1, p. 62, and below, Appendix 2, pp. 85-8).

method of bringing home to the road user the costs that he can at present effectively ignore, although in arriving at its unit charge the corporation would no doubt have to experiment.

Some resistance to such an idea might be expected, although its equitability should be a point in its favour with the motoring and trade associations. It would of course enable local authority rates to be substantially reduced. Even though this would probably be offset to some extent by increased transport costs being passed on to the consumer, the burden upon the householder would be lessened. Doubtless the petrol tax would remain, but it would have become a manifest form of sumptuary taxation except to the extent that it was used as an instrument of energy policy. The result would be not only to place transport policy on a more rational basis, but also to produce a far fairer and more honest system than the hybrid we have today.

This two-part structure follows broadly the recommendations of the Allais Report,[1] which also envisaged that the congestion tax element would both signal a demand for further investment and accumulate funds for the purpose. A side benefit would be that the under-employment of rural roads would be recognised, the rural user remaining exempt from the congestion tax until he ventured onto a busy main road or into a town.

If the logic of the Allais Report were followed and infrastructure pricing were to become a tool for optimising the use of existing investment and identifying where more was required, the next step would be to give 'British Roads' responsibility for the railway infrastructure as well, turning it into a National Track Corporation. It is no doubt asking a good deal of railway traditionalists to accept such an idea, but it is to be hoped they will not reject it out of hand—it could in practice lead to the return of traffic to the railways without central direction, and considerably ease their investment problems as well.

In a country innately suspicious of bold and imaginative innovations, it may be too much to expect that such a corporation, with or without its railway side, could come into existence. But the introduction of market-based pricing for the transport infrastructure is of paramount importance, and it

[1] *Options for Transport Tariff Policy,* HMSO, 1965 (also above, p. 49).

would be a heroic assumption that either local or central government could be entrusted with its administration. A new self-financing corporation charged with such a duty might just achieve the desired result. Perhaps the parallel with the BBC is illuminating—including the same requirement to maintain the independence of the corporation from ministerial control and interference.

THE FUTURE OF PUBLIC ENTERPRISE

The extent to which the state transport organisations—British Airways, British Rail, the National Bus Company, the Scottish Transport Group, the British Airports Authority and the Docks Board—distort the market in their respective spheres is debatable. What should concern us is not a doctrinaire notion of 'reprivatisation' so much as the element of monopoly which would remain even if a state board was turned into a quoted public company. It would be equally wrong to make a rigid commitment to the supposed benefits of one particular alternative; small private businesses are not immune from the desire for a quiet life. Moreover, the potential of co-ownership firms, autonomous work groups, and self-help organisations must not be neglected.

Divorcing British Rail from the state

The history of the railways has been one of centralisation. Here, again, it may be too much of an emotional leap to consider the possibility of reversing the trend. A successful attempt was, however, made in the 1960s; the decentralising process begun then by Sir Reginald Wilson in the Eastern Region has continued to give more power and responsibility to management in the field. If responsibility for rail track was transferred to a national corporation, it would be logical to carry the process further, identifying 'labyrinths' which could be both cost centres and the focus for 'house loyalty'. It would also be logical for the 'labyrinths' to compete for traffic where such a potential still exists—chiefly in the freight market (as the subsidiaries of the road freight holding company, Transport Development Group, compete). The shape of such a 'federal railway' is one that merits serious consideration—most of all by railwaymen (of all grades).

Organisation is not, however, the only obstacle to returning

[69]

the railways to market disciplines. In the background lies the issue of finance. So long as railway administration is dependent upon state funds to increase its investment capital, to renew its assets, and even to reduce the scale of its operations in order to make economies, so long must it remain within the penumbra of government. Again, there would seem to be advantages in giving a track corporation responsibility for that part of BR's operations labelled 'track and signalling', which would give it an opportunity to apply the Allais concept of charging. As with the roads, a two-part tariff would be developed. But since much railway track is currently under-used, the 'quasi-rent' element would not apply (at least not until sufficient traffic had been attracted to rail to increase its use).

A further benefit would be the incentive to railway management to take a more entrepreneurial attitude towards their business than in the past, when the allocation of infrastructure costs has absorbed so much of their attention.

The impetus to decentralisation in buses

Decentralisation is already in progress in bus transport. In recent years the National Bus Company has examined its own operations using a technique christened the market analysis programme (MAP), which focusses upon a much smaller unit of production than the traditional area agreement company.[1] A typical MAP area will be the labyrinth of services that centre upon a small town, although the technique can be applied to conurbations and to long-distance services. The MAP technique has been criticised on methodological grounds because it stops short of market research proper, and on practical grounds because it does not develop new traffic. But its concentration upon the 'micro' problems of bus operation opens up new possibilities for the bus industry.

One NBC subsidiary, Midland Red, has now been re-organised around the MAP areas. It is easy to imagine the state-owned buses being run entirely by management at this level, drawing upon strategically placed centres for major engineering support and management services. This development would be a logical consequence of abandoning territorial cross-subsidisation, which brought the area agreement com-

---

[1] The area agreement companies are the subsidiaries of the National Bus Company and the Scottish Bus Group, which are the 'household names' of the bus industry.

panies into being, and it would further undermine the rationale of the quantity licensing system introduced to protect their monopolies.

The National Bus Company and its Scottish equivalent should be encouraged to proceed along these lines, on the understanding that each 'labyrinth' must justify itself financially. Further deregulation[1] would require each local unit to stand on its own feet (or wheels), with independent units—many of which exist already—developing as part of the pattern. Signs of a bureaucratic preoccupation with tidiness would have to be resisted; and the system must be open to change, having both actual and potential competition built into it. The state corporations might, of course, be encouraged in time to dispose of some or all of their operating units, though that would not necessarily be desirable; both the NBC and the Scottish Bus Group have considerable expertise at their disposal, which their operating units could draw upon to the advantage of their customers, and which by no means all independent units could possess.

Reprivatising the two corporations is an option to be treated with caution, since it could produce a considerable concentration of power. But this is not inevitable; the structure could be designed to produce a series of medium-sized holding companies, similar in style to the Transport Development Group in the freight sector.[2]

The remainder of the public sector consists of municipal enterprise, including that of the Metropolitan County Councils, the GLC, and the hybrid Greater Glasgow Passenger Transport Executive. There is no reason why, over much of the country, municipal enterprise should not have its place at the local level, alongside the state-owned units and the independents (which might include co-operatives and self-help groups of various kinds). The real problem begins to emerge in the larger cities and conurbations, where the size of unit is currently determined by the local authority area, and not by the optimum fleet size. Optimum fleet size is almost certainly considerably smaller than that produced by many municipal boundaries.

---

[1] Such as that suggested in the author's earlier Hobart Paper 23, *Transport for Passengers, op. cit.*

[2] An alternative might be a structure resembling what has emerged in France and the USA, where former operators have returned as managing agents for local authorities.

It is these areas which require road-use pricing most acutely, since they already suffer the worst congestion because of the failure of the present system of road finance to take account of the scarcity of urban land. Yet it would be rash to assume that such a reform would be sufficient to eradicate the problems of urban transport; the retention of some form of administrative oversight seems essential, at least in the short run. A Conurbation Transport Authority (CTA), with responsibility for investment in the infrastructure (perhaps delegated from a national track corporation), would have to have surveillance over the transport operators in both road and rail. But there is no reason why it should own them.

The geographical scope and composition of CTAs would have to be carefully thought out. Experience with local government reform over the past 10 years makes it plain that local authority areas are not necessarily appropriate to the requirements of urban transport. Under the Local Government Act of 1972, Coventry was included in the West Midlands metropolitan county for reasons quite unrelated to transport policy which would instead have required it be located in an authority along the axis of Nuneaton-Coventry-Kenilworth-Leamington. The same Act excluded Redditch and Cannock, although both are more closely associated than Coventry with transport in the West Midlands.

It therefore seems that any development of CTAs would have to be on an *ad hoc* basis, a suggestion which experience with the Water Authorities will immediately prejudice. Yet the original Passenger Transport Authorities established under the Transport Act of 1968 were very effective bodies. And the system that was devised then of permitting the local authorities in each PTA area to nominate its members may be the best (though democratic purists might disagree). Public opinion must have a say through the ballot box in decisions of such widespread concern. But consumers will be denied the major benefits the market has to offer if the result is to politicise transport.

Network of CTAs to control infrastructure and oversee public transport

What is envisaged, therefore, is a number of state bodies encompassing the larger urban areas—to include cities like

[72]

Bristol and Nottingham, as well as the Scottish and Welsh conurbations—which would combine responsibility for infrastructure with the oversight of public transport. To integrate all transport modes into the same policy framework, these bodies would have the duty of developing some form of road-use pricing, including parking. Their overseeing responsibilities would extend to freight transport and distribution,[1] perhaps through the requirement that all holders of an operator's licence should co-operate with the CTAs in matters of access and congestion. No doubt the CTAs would require a carefully drawn remit so as to prevent them from falling back upon the criterion of 'the public interest', which of all concepts is the most likely to stifle competition and innovation.

Within the CTA areas, the form of decentralisation might vary. Local units having access to central services at a higher level (discussed on pp. 70-1)—based perhaps upon autonomous work groups responsible for individual routes—are a possibility. They might develop into true co-ownership units, similar to the Mondragon structure in northern Spain. There is a considerable reservoir of managerial talent for relatively small-scale operations which is wasted in the large units of today. Furthermore, 'house loyalty' is a considerable asset to units small enough for both employees and customers to identify with. The National Bus Company still serves some conurbations (Bristol, the Potteries, and parts of Merseyside and Tyneside), and the sort of decentralisation already suggested for its operations might be appropriate in such areas.

Intervention to encourage decentralisation in cities

Whereas over much of the country the removal of quantity control might be sufficient to trigger the process of change to a more flexible and demand-responsive system, the existing concentration of ownership in the larger cities and conurbations would require a more interventionist policy. Each new CTA might be given the initial duty of encouraging decentralisation in whatever form seemed desirable. With this in mind, it would be sensible for central government to take powers,

---

[1] It is usual to distinguish between freight transport, which is the movement of goods for industry, and distribution, which is the movement of foodstuffs and finished products to the shops.

as Mrs Castle did with the PTAs, to appoint a small number of the members of the CTAs.

Once the system was established, however, the duties of the CTAs would be similar to those already possessed by the non-metropolitan county councils (which would retain them in areas outside the remit of the CTAs). Decentralised railway units would, of course, be subject to the same authority.

V. CONCLUSIONS AND RECOMMENDATIONS FOR POLICY

This *Paper* is directed not only to economists and others with an interest in the principles involved, but also to the personnel of the transport industry with whom the author has shared his career. Three parties have an interest in a healthy transport industry: its customers and potential customers (which effectively means everyone); those who work in it or own a bit of it; and society as a whole, which must be concerned with its external costs and benefits and the use it makes of scarce resources with alternative uses. Each group will stand to benefit from a market-oriented industry free from political intervention and subject to the minimum of administrative control.

If such an objective can be attained, externalities and difficulties of allocation can be tackled in a rational manner, without undue pressure from vested interests. The reform of infrastructure pricing would be particularly beneficial in this respect and, together with a minimum of quantity control, must be the economic goal of policy. These improvements, together with the decentralisation of management, can offer public transport a viable future, with a reasonable return on its investment. They will also make it a better industry to work in. If they introduce an element of risk at the same time, they also hold out the prospect of a return of freedom to managers to take decisions and the opportunity for staff to belong to smaller, more human units of operation. Above all, a healthy public transport industry offers job security, which is by no means certain if things continue as they are.

The widespread pessimism about the industry today stems from the belief that heavy (and indeed increasing) subsidies will continue to be necessary, a belief that defies reason. For, as railwaymen know, the moment arrives in a democracy when opportunity costs are brought to book and, through its representatives, the community decides it would rather spend the subsidies on other activities—on schools, hospitals, police, or whatever. At that point, policies aimed at protecting employment have become self-defeating. It is this argument which

[75]

ought to convince trade unionists (of whom the author is one) that their best interest lies in minimising the influence of government over public transport.

The essential function of the industry is to make its living by serving the consumer, a truism which a protectionist mentality originating in the inter-war years succeeded for some time in concealing. Management today has moved a long way from the 'sneering condescension' which in 1932 greeted a reminder from Sir Arnold Plant that protectionism impoverishes the consumer.[1] The concluding remarks of this *Paper* will thus be addressed to the new generation of managers, from whom the author has gathered many of the insights which, hopefully, it contains.

Structural reform is not enough. Moreover, there has been too much of it already in the past 60 years. What is proposed here is no more than is necessary to make the industry competitive and efficient. Central government would retain responsibility for quality regulation through the existing operator's licence, administered by the Traffic Commissioners, while an absolute minimum of quantity control would be left with Conurbation Transport Authorities and, elsewhere, the county councils. Subsidies from state funds are not ruled out; but cross-subsidisation would stop, and the cost of direct subsidies would become transparent. It is probable that the recommendations of this *Paper* would so restore the health of public transport as to minimise the need for subsidies anyway. But this is not a blueprint for Utopia; rather it is an attempt to free the mechanisms of the market to satisfy the wide range of demand in a prosperous economy.

Achieving this goal depends upon the willingness of all with an interest in the transport industry accepting new ideas—and putting them into practice. Not every busman, railwayman, local councillor or trade unionist will find them easy to take on board. But the alternative is massive and growing subsidies

---

[1] Mr Arnold Plant, as he then was, had contributed a paper to the Institute of Transport (now the Chartered Institute of Transport) entitled 'Co-ordination and Competition in Transport' (*Journal of the Institute of Transport*, Vol. 13, No. 3, 1932), in which he pointed out the potential effect of the then new system of bus licensing in 'impoverishing the consumer'. Plant's standing as a member of staff of the London School of Economics did not protect him from the 'sneering condescension' of men like Lord Ashfield (the founder of London Transport) and Brigadier Sir Osborne Mance. (Stuart Joy, *The Train that Ran Away*, Ian Allan, Shepperton, Middlesex, 1973, p.27.)

—in some European cities public transport derives only 25 per cent of its revenue from fares. It is arguable, to say the least, that transfer payments on this scale (already contemplated in some parts of the UK) are inequitable, and there are sound reasons to believe that they damage the efficient management of public transport fleets. They undoubtedly benefit the wealthy suburbs rather than the deprived inner-city areas (where bus services tend to be more fully used and profitable). Above all, they imply monopoly; since 1930 monopoly has proved incapable of ensuring either high standards of service to the public or financial success.

A programme for action

The general conclusion of this *Hobart Paper* is that there has been too much government of transport during the past 60 years, and that a return to the self-regulation of the market will be to the advantage of all whose interest is identified with a healthy transport industry: those who use it, those who work in it, and those who are affected by its problems of allocation and externalities. The control of transport by politicians has become excessive and ought to be diminished.

That this statement is true most emphatically in railways and bus services reflects the statutory protection they have enjoyed for so long to enable them to practise cross-subsidisation. It is cross-subsidisation that has blunted their competitive edge, producing the common fallacy that they are inevitably loss-makers. It has also enabled British Rail and the large publicly-owned bus operators to grow far beyond their probable optimum size, and to pursue policies which frequently harm the three interested parties identified above.

A programme of reform follows under three main headings: the pricing of the infrastructure ('track, terminals and signalling'); the decentralisation of ownership; and the return to certain well-tried market-oriented practices. The three require to be pursued in parallel.

1. *The central issue—pricing the transport infrastructure (track)*

A corporation (with the suggested title of 'British Roads') should take over the ownership and management of the roads from central and local government. It should be self-financing (and able to borrow at commercial rates), obtaining its revenue from

(a) a vehicle tax based on the physical costs imposed by each class of vehicle, and

(b) a variety of road-use pricing schemes designed to reflect the element of congestion.

Petrol tax would become what it truly is—a sumptuary tax levied on a commodity for which demand is highly inelastic (it could also be legitimately used as an arm of energy policy). There is also a strong argument for making the corporation a complete track authority, vesting in it ownership of the infrastructure ('track') of the railways (both British Rail and London Transport). But it is probably more important to establish a rational basis for *road* finance since, without it, further reforms are likely to be undermined by the distortions in the present system whereby scarce road space has a marginal price of zero.

2. *The treatment of public enterprise: removing institutional rigidities*

So-called 'reprivatisation' is not equivalent to a return to the market. To transfer the express coach services of the National Bus Company to a private owner (as is now proposed) would leave its successor in exactly the same position of market dominance. The cautious deregulation introduced in the Transport Act of 1980 should be taken further, leaving only the quality licence and a minimum route-licensing system, which experience might then show to be unnecessary. But the existing structure of public transport is so centralised that to wait for market forces to change it would not be enough; the institutional rigidities are such that this might never happen. A guideline exists for decentralising management responsibility to the level where market information is readily available and market forces could come into play.

The cost centres for public transport tend to take the form of relatively small 'labyrinths' (except in urban bus operation where they are the individual services). Already in the National Bus Company there is a move to restructure management in recognition of this fact. An immediate step should be to wind down the 'territorial' bus companies and transfer their operations to smaller units, each drawing upon one of a limited number of centres providing technical support and management services.[1] After all, the territorial companies were explicitly intended to be instruments of cross-subsidisation and, as such, are both undesirable and anachronistic. The same arguments apply to both British Rail and air transport, and similar devolution should be introduced there (the arguments against it are likely to be rooted in historical prejudice). The air transport industry, however, really ought to be seen as part of a competitive market for the whole of Europe.

True cross-subsidisation—which arises when operations that fail to cover their escapable costs (which may be very low) are continued beyond the short term—produces economic distortions and tends to be regressive. Blanket subsidies from public funds most frequently benefit those who need them least. When the forces of the market have been given full play and the remaining element of personal hardship in terms of 'access' has been minimised, there may be circumstances where public funds should be employed to provide a better quality of service, usually in the form of higher frequency. One of the advantages of the market is that such intervention becomes far easier to cost and control, though techniques require to be developed to avoid inhibiting market mechanisms.

There is, however, reason to suppose that the market is not fully effective in its optimising role in urban transport, where the factor of land is in such short supply that the price mechanism alone is of doubtful value as a regulator. Road-use pricing is one method of tackling that problem, but it is not a panacea. During the big transport debate of the 1960s, which produced the unwieldy Passenger Transport Authorities with their arbitrary boundaries, it was suggested that public bodies should be established to co-ordinate land-use and transport policies in the main urban areas. This *Paper* recommends such Conurbation Transport Authorities for all major urban areas, the areas to be determined by the requirements of transport policy and not by local government boundaries (though a substantial number of their members should be nominated by the appropriate local authorities). In addition to their duties of co-ordination, they should initially be responsible for dismantling the existing monopolies—along

[1] Such centres could also sell their services to private firms in both passenger and freight transport.

[79]

lines not dissimilar to those suggested above for the National Bus Company. (A diversity of operating units should be encouraged, including community-based systems, co-operatives and autonomous work groups as well as small entrepreneurial companies. They might well compete with each other. Some might run trains.)

3. *Some new initiatives*

In addition to such restructuring—which should be the last for a very long time—this *Paper* considers two aspects of current management practice to be in urgent need of change. In each the heavy hand of regulation has caused distortions which must be corrected to ensure they do not inhibit market forces.

The first is to abandon standard charging in favour of a pricing policy for bus transport that reflects the way demand elasticities vary. The National Bus Company is already moving in this direction, and the dismantling of price control following the Transport Act of 1980 has shown some operators what advantages there are in pricing according to the market. But it is in urban transport that the principle of standard charging is still most deeply entrenched. There it is a consequence of the ill-considered belief that it is equitable to charge the same rate per mile throughout the system, irrespective of variations in cost or in price or income elasticity of demand. (Standard charging, as a concomitant of cross-subsidisation, is also regressive in its effect.) An early duty of the Conurbation Transport Authorities should be to encourage management to recognise that variable charging is in everyone's interest.

The second major shift should be away from the large buses introduced over the past 25 years in a misguided search for higher labour productivity. Both theory and overseas practice indicate that small, frequent buses are sufficiently preferred by the consumer to generate a positive cash flow. There is no advantage in doubling the size of buses if the consequence is drastically to reduce their frequency and hence the quality of the service they provide. The combination of smaller buses and higher frequency might well lead to more than one set of price and quality on the same route, thus increasing the likelihood of the maximum satisfaction of demand.

Finally, it is to be hoped that the reforms proposed in this

[80]

Paper will be accepted in the spirit in which they are offered—an earnest attempt to make public transport work better for the consumer, and to make it a better place to work in, while at the same time tackling the underlying problems that governments have ignored for too long.

There is no justification for the convention that assumes transport to be in some way unsuited to the disciplines of the market. As an alternative, the administrative solution has proved itself bankrupt, unable even to ensure satisfaction to those who work in the industry. Without making excessive claims for the market as a panacea, it must be accepted that the trend of policy over the past 60 years has been accompanied by ever-growing problems. During the whole of this period the government of transport has been widened and strengthened, but the time has now come to put an end to over-government and to harness the neglected advantages of the market economy.

APPENDIX 1

Summary of Inland Transport Legislation, 1920 to 1980

1920 *Railways Act*—Consolidated the 120 railway companies into four, each representing a 'system' rather than a 'territory'.

1924 *London Traffic Act*—Introduced quantity control of bus operations in London in an attempt to protect the 'combine', and especially the tramways of both the combine and the LCC. (The 'combine' was the loose grouping of firms that surrounded the London Electric Railway Company, which itself owned the London General Omnibus Company. Its monopoly had been broken by the 'pirates' whose buses had appeared on the streets of London in 1922.)

1926 *Motor Vehicles (Traffic & Regulations) Act (Northern Ireland)*— Took away licensing powers from local authorities, and opened up Belfast to competition. New regulations followed in 1928 giving existing operators in the Province a 'franchise' and prohibiting new services.

1930 *Road Traffic Act*—Extended quantity control, and added price control, to all bus and coach operations in Britain in an attempt to protect the railways and the municipal and territorial bus operators (and tramways).

1933 *London Passenger Transport Act*—Effectively converted the combine into a public board (there being no change in the senior management) with compulsory acquisition of all the other operators (except the main-line railways, whose suburban services were not affected). The LCC thus lost its tramway undertaking. This is often called 'Morrison's Act', but in fact he voted against it.

1933 *Road & Rail Traffic Act*—Introduced quantity control of public road haulage (not 'own-account') in a conscious attempt to protect the railways and the handful of large public hauliers.

1935 *Road & Railway Transport Act (Northern Ireland)*—Set up the Northern Ireland Road Transport Board with compulsory acquisition of virtually all road passenger and freight operators in the Province (except for Belfast City Transport), including the road fleets of the railways.

[82]

1947 *Transport Act*—The nationalising act, setting up the British Transport Commission (BTC) and its Executives (one of them being London Transport); compulsory acquisition of railways, canals, docks and public haulage (but not 'own-account'); provision for 'Area Schemes' to re-organise bus and coach operations, with powers of compulsory purchase. After the Act's passage, the Tilling and Scottish bus groups were sold voluntarily to the BTC, which also acquired the railway shareholdings in the British Electric Traction (BET) companies.

1948 *Transport Act (Northern Ireland)* — Merged the state-owned road operations and most of the railways in the Province to form the Ulster Transport Authority (UTA).

1953 *Transport Act*—The denationalising act, with disposal of the BTC's road haulage fleet (never completed), abolition of the Executives, and termination of 'Area Schemes'.

1956 *Transport Act*—Re-organised the railways, creating Boards for each Region with outside directors.

1962 *Transport Act*—Abolished the BTC, setting up Boards (e.g. British Railways Board (BR) and London Transport Board), with a Transport Holding Company for state-owned buses and lorries.

1966 *Transport Act (Northern Ireland)*—Set up a licensing system for road freight transport and relieved UTA of monopoly powers and duties.

1967 *Transport Act (Northern Ireland)*—Abolished the UTA, setting up a Transport Holding Company to own a Northern Ireland Railways Company Ltd. and road passenger operations, including Belfast City services. Set up quantity licensing for buses and modified the freight licensing system.

1968 *Transport Act*—Major re-organisation (Mrs Castle's Act): quantity control of road haulage abandoned; state-owned road haulage became National Freight Corporation; state-owned bus and coach operations (now including BET companies) re-organised as National Bus Company and (with Scottish shipping services) Scottish Transport Group; four Passenger Transport Authorities (PTAs) set up with wide powers including compulsory acquisition, and automatic acquisition of municipal fleets in their areas; duties of co-operation between road and rail operators.

[83]

1969 *Transport (London) Act*—Transferred London Transport to GLC with debts written off, but did not create a PTA (i.e. BR services left out).

1972 *Local Government Act*—Transport consequences included creation of two new PTAs and modification of boundaries of others, and their transformation into municipal transport departments of Metropolitan County Councils; co-ordinating powers and duties to 'shire' County Councils.

1980 *Transport Act*—Abandoned quantity control of coach services over 30 miles; virtually abandoned price control for all bus and coach services; shifted onus of proof onto objectors in remaining (bus) quantity control; provided for experimental areas (rural in practice) with removal of quantity control.

APPENDIX 2

Vehicle Metering Devices for Road-use Pricing:
*A Summary of the Smeed Report's Findings**

In 1962, the Minister of Transport appointed a committee of engineers, economists and traffic experts under the chairmanship of [the late] Professor R. J. Smeed 'To study and report on the technical feasibility of various methods of improving the pricing system relating to the use of roads, and on relevant economic considerations.' This committee reported its findings in the summer of 1963, and its report was published in 1964 under the title *Road Pricing: the Economic and Technical Possibilities*.[1]

The Smeed Committee's examination of charging methods was based on 17 'operational requirements for a road pricing system'. The following points cover the most important:

Charges should be flexible and closely related to the amount of use made of the roads. People who often use congested roads should pay more for them than those who do not. This could be achieved by making the charges proportional to distance travelled on congested roads, or to the time spent on them. It should be possible to vary the charges as between periods of peak congestion and other times, and to allow road use at very little charge when there is no congestion, i.e. at night. Vehicles causing heavy congestion—lorries, for example—should be charged more.

Another important requirement is that intending drivers should be able to discover the charges payable before making a journey, as the object of road pricing is to influence the decision of people *before* they use congested roads, and therefore any system that imposed heavy charges without giving prior warning would fail in its main purpose. The charging method should be cheap to work, easily enforceable, and acceptable to the public as being simple and fair. The state should not have to issue invoices to millions of road users nor become responsible for debt collection. Payment in advance would therefore be essential except in rare cases. Equipment should be secure, robust and reliable. There would be no room for delicate instrumentation. The system should be capable of nationwide installation and provision must be made for it to

---

*Reprinted from G. J. Roth, *A Self-financing Road System*, Research Monograph 3, IEA, 1966, pp. 48-51. Mr Roth was a member of the Smeed Committee.
[1] HMSO, 1964.

[85]

accommodate an estimated vehicle population of 30 million by the end of the century.

The system should preferably be applicable to charging parked as well as moving vehicles so that it could take the place of parking meters, and reduce enforcement and collection costs. It should also allow for occasional users such as visitors from abroad and car users who visit priced areas only rarely. These people should be covered by the scheme with the minimum of formality and delay.

Finally, and perhaps most important from one viewpoint, the charging method should indicate the strength of demand for road space in different places and at different times of day, and it should enable the payments made over alternative routes to be known in some detail.

The first requirement, that charges should be closely related to the use of congested roads, makes it necessary to have a meter. The Smeed Committee considered two types:

(i) *Off-vehicle meters:* remote control units actuated *by* vehicles but situated at a central computing station. This type of meter can be compared to telephone meters.

(ii) *On-vehicle meters:* meters designed to record *on* vehicles. This type of meter can be compared to taxi meters.

Off-vehicle meters are more costly than on-vehicle ones, and as they had no special advantages they were rejected. But the Committee described six on-vehicle meter systems which, it considered, might be developed into charging methods capable of fulfilling most of the operational requirements. The metering systems recommended for further study can be divided into two types: 'point pricing' and 'continuous pricing'. Under point pricing, vehicles would be charged as and when they pass fixed pricing points which would activate their meters. Under continuous pricing, vehicles would be charged while within pricing zones.

Point pricing

The meter carried by the vehicle under point pricing would count electrical impulses generated by electrical cables carrying very low currents and laid across the road at the pricing points. The cables would be energised all the time so that any vehicle passing over them would receive the appropriate impulse. (Provision could be made to ensure that any vehicle stopping over the cable would not receive more than one impulse.) Impulse transmitting cables need not be laid singly; they could be laid in groups of, say, 5 or 10, and so arranged that either the full number or only some of the cables would be energised at any one time.

The vehicle meter would probably be the size and shape of a small book. It would be near the ground to pick up the signals and could form part of the number plate. In its simplest form, the meter would probably be in the form of a 'solid state' counter, of the form used in computers.[1]

Two methods of payment are possible. Either a meter could be sold with a given capacity and exchanged when exhausted, or else the meter could be fixed permanently to the vehicle and taken at intervals to authorised meter stations to be read and paid for. In both cases there would be no difficulty about pre-payment. Meters might cost £5 to £15 depending on the visual indication provided and the road equipment might be approximately £250 per pricing point. The number of pricing points required to cover the whole of Britain was estimated to be 20,000.[2]

Continuous pricing

Under systems of continuous pricing, pricing zones would have to be designated, and vehicles would be charged according to the time or distance travelled in those zones. The main problems are how to switch the meters on and off at the entrances to the zones, and how to obtain payment.

Switching the meters on or off could be done either manually by the driver or automatically by electrical impulses transmitted at the borders of the pricing zones. In both cases meters of this kind would have to carry a light or some other indication to show when they are switched on. It would be possible to have different zones, for example, high-priced 'red' zones in the most congested areas and lower-priced 'blue' zones in less congested areas. Charges could be varied with the time of the day: a zone could be 'red' during the peak traffic hours, 'blue' during the rest of the day and free at night. In that case the meters could be made to show a red light when in a 'red' zone ,and a blue light when in a 'blue' zone.

Payment could be made by means of electrical timers. The pricing meters could receive their main power supply from car batteries, but the connection to the battery could be by means of a sealed unit incorporating a relay. This relay would only effect a connection if a special kind of battery or other electrical timer was inserted into a slot to activate the relay. The battery could be similar to a coin in size and shape and would be designed to actuate the relay for a minimum number of hours. In the case of different prices

---

[1] The 'solid state' counter has no moving parts nor does it show any visible sign of counting; it consists of a number of segments which can be electrically charged or discharged and in that way it can count in binary numbers. Although such a meter could not be read in the ordinary way, it could be made to change colour when exhausted, or when almost exhausted, and in that way would show whether it was run down.

[2] This figure may be compared with the number of road intersections controlled by traffic lights of which there are about 4,000.

[87]

being set for different pricing zones, it would be possible to arrange for the timing unit to last for, say, 10 hours in a 'blue' zone or, say, 5 hours in a 'red' zone.

The batteries, or other types of electrical timers, could be sold through garages and ordinary shops, the road congestion tax being included in their price. By skilful design of the battery and the meter it would be possible to make it difficult and expensive to forge the electrical timing units.

Another possibility would be to use a clockwork timer. This would have to be wound up—or exchanged—when run down, on payment of the appropriate road charge at an authorised depot.

The possible cost would be 30s. for a manual meter, £3 to £5 for an automatic one and £10 for a clockwork one. The electric timing units might possibly cost between 1s. and 2s. each and the road equipment for the automatic meters £50 per point.

The technical conclusions of the Smeed Report have not, to my knowledge, been challenged, and it may therefore be assumed that there are no major technical difficulties in charging road prices which would roughly approximate to the congestion costs imposed by vehicles on other road users. The costs of such systems would be small compared to the benefits that are estimated to result from their use.

APPENDIX 3

A Summary of the Relevant Literature

The Institute of Economic Affairs has published a significant contribution to the debate on transport policy. The author's Hobart Paper 23, *Transport for Passengers,* was published in 1963, with a revised edition in 1971. Mr Gabriel Roth's Hobart Paper 33, *Paying for Parking,* appeared in 1965, and the issues covered in the present study were thoroughly explored in the late Gilbert Ponsonby's Hobart Paper 49, *Transport Policy: Co-ordination through Competition,* in 1969. Mr Roth also wrote a Research Monograph (No. 3), *A Self-financing Road System,* in 1966, and this was followed in 1968 by Professor A. A. Walter's Research Monograph No. 15, *Integration in Freight Transport*; in the same year Mr D. J. Reynolds's Research Report, *Economics, Town Planning and Traffic,* was published. Mr Samuel Brittan's Hobart Paperback No. 2, *Government and the Market Economy* (1971), briefly discusses the state transport undertakings and their monopoly, and touches upon standard charging (pp. 36-38).

Much useful background material will be found in an article by Dr D. F. Channon, 'Strategy, Structure and Political Intervention in the Land-based Nationalised Transport System' (*Business Archives,* No. 41, January 1976). Reference has already been made (pp. 37-8) to Dr J. A. Crowley's article 'Competition in Air Transport' (*Journal of Irish Business and Administrative Research,* Dublin, Vol. 3, No. 1, April 1981), which has significant implications for competition within other modes of transport. Recent articles in the *Journal of Transport Economics and Policy* (*JTEP*) which have far-reaching implications for urban transport in particular, deserve close attention. Among them, and also referred to already (p. 61), is 'Optimal Service Frequency and Bus Size' by Mr J. O. Jansson, which gives theoretical underpinning to the argument that buses are now too large—and infrequent (*JTEP,* Vol. XIV, No. 1, January 1980). It was followed by two articles by Professor Philip A. Viton of the University of Pennsylvania: 'The Possibility of Profitable Bus Service' (*JTEP,* Vol. XIV, No. 3, September 1980) and 'Privately Provided Urban Transport Services' (JTEP, Vol. XVI, No. 1, January 1982). They deal weighty blows to the conventional wisdom that subsidisation of transport is inevitable and competition dangerous. Professor Viton enters the important disclaimer that his conclusions have no bearing upon the issue of replacing public service

[89]

carriers by private firms. But his contributions are refreshingly different from the traditional thinking about urban transport.

It is sad that so much work done on each side of the Atlantic fails to overcome the barrier of ocean. Recent material relevant to the present *Paper* includes Mr Gabriel Roth's article, 'Economics of a Unified Transportation Trust Fund' (National Academy of Sciences, *Transportation Research Record*, No. 731, 1979), and the World Bank Staff Working Paper, 'Ownership and Efficiency in Urban Buses', by Mr C. Feibel and Professor Walters, published in 1980.

The conclusions of the present *Paper* about the reform of infrastructure finance were reached before the publication of Mr Roth's valuable 'Financial Profitability as an Investment Criterion for Transport Projects', which challenges the accepted orthodoxy along similar lines. Mr Roth's paper was presented to the 1981 International Symposium on Surface Transportation Performance and was published the same year by the US Department of Transportation in the proceedings of the Symposium. It deserves the attention of all who accept the need for a more rational policy.

Also of considerable interest is *Transit Pricing Techniques to Improve Productivity*, a report published in 1979 by the US Department of Transportation. And a useful study of the economics of cross-subsidisation can be found in Chapter 5 of *The Intercity Bus Industry*, a preliminary study issued by the Inter-state Commerce Commission in 1978.

Practice in transport varies less in different countries throughout the world than might be expected, as the present author's current research is showing. Pending publication of this research, some information may be obtained from the report, *Competition Policy in Regulated Sectors*, published by the OECD in 1979.

TOPICS FOR DISCUSSION

1. What are the principal arguments advanced against leaving transport to the market? Do you think transport is 'special'?

2. 'Economists in general, and for good reason, regard cross-subsidisation rather as parsons regard sin.' Why?

3. Are there good economic reasons for maintaining administrative control over passenger transport when it is not thought necessary for the carriage of goods (except to enforce safety standards)?

4. Explain how the dispute about economies of scale in transport affects the case for leaving it to the market.

5. 'Part of the case for a market solution lies in its ability to *minimise* the cost of any subvention and to indicate objectively at which point it should be applied.' Discuss, with examples from recent transport history.

6. Is there a more 'efficient' way of ensuring that poor people can afford public transport than by subsidising its price?

7. What are the economic drawbacks of large, double-deck buses?

8. The author suggests there should be 'Sainsbury' and 'Quicksave' buses, and various other brand names in between, all catering for different segments of the market and operating at a profit like their supermarket equivalents. Do you agree and, if so, why?

9. 'That the price of using the infrastructure is zero at the margin cannot make sense with something so scarce as urban road space.' Explain.

10. Evaluate critically the author's proposal for pricing road use by a two-part tariff.

FURTHER READING

Bendixson, T., *Instead of Cars,* Penguin edition (revised, 1977).

Bonavia, M. R., *British Rail – The First 25 Years,* David & Charles, 1981.

——, *Railway Policy between the Wars,* Manchester University Press, 1981.

Cresswell, R. (ed.), *Rural Transport and Country Planning,* Leonard Hill, 1978.

Dunn, J. A., Jr., *Miles to Go: European and American Transportation Policies,* MIT Press, Cambridge, Mass., 1981.

El-Agraa, A. M. (ed.), *The Economics of the European Community* (Chapter 8, 'The Transport Policy', by K. M. Gwilliam), Philip Allan, Oxford, 1980.

Glaister, S., *Fundamentals of Transport Economics,* Blackwell, Oxford, 1981.

Gourvish, T. R., *Railways and the British Economy, 1830-1914,* Macmillan, London, 1980.

Gwilliam, K. M., & Mackie, P. J., *Economics and Transport Policy,* George Allen & Unwin, London, 1975.

Hensher, D. A., (ed.), *Urban Transport Economics,* Cambridge University Press, London, 1977.

Hibbs, J., *The Bus and Coach Industry –Its Economics and Organisation,* J. M. Dent, London, 1975.

Hillman, M. *et al., Personal Mobility and Transport Policy,* PEP, London, 1973.

Hillman M., & Whalley, A., *Walking* is *Transport,* Policy Studies Institute, London, 1979.

Hutchins, J. G. B., *Transportation and the Environment,* Paul Elek, London, 1977.

Nash, C. A., *Public versus Private Transport,* Macmillan, London, 1976.

Nuffield Foundation, *A Policy for Transport?,* 1977.

Pryke, R. W. S., & Dodgson, J. S., *The Rail Problem,* Martin Robertson, London, 1975.

Shaw, S., *Air Transport – A Marketing Perspective,* Pitman, 1982.

Starkie, D. N. M., *Transportation Planning, Policy and Analysis,* Pergamon, Oxford, 1976.

——, *The Motorway Age – Road and Traffic Policies in Post-war Britain,* Pergamon, Oxford, 1982.

Stubbs, P. C., Tyson, W. J., & Dalvi, M. Q., *Transport Economics,* George Allen & Unwin, London, 1980.

White, P. R., *Planning for Public Transport,* Hutchinson, London, 1976.

Other IEA Books Available on Transport

Research Monograph 3

A Self-financing Road System

G. J. ROTH

1966   50 pence

'The principle of user cost pricing is well argued by G. J. Roth. . . . envisages that charges would be made to vehicle users and also cyclists and pedestrians, according to the use they make; to public utilities who use road reservations for their mains; to car parkers who use the highway for standing space, by night as well as day.'

NATHANIEL LICHFIELD, *The Times*

'All transport men should certainly study the *Monograph* closely, for although the proposals might seem far-fetched they could well influence the thinking of the strengthened MoT economics section.' *Modern Transport*

Research Monograph 15

Integration in Freight Transport

A. A. WALTERS

1968   60 pence

Background Memorandum 2

Contrasts in Nationalised Transport Since 1947

GEORGE POLANYI

1968   £1·00

'This Memorandum singles out the record of nationalised transport during 20 years in which the tug-of-war between commercial and social (and political) criteria has pulled railway management first one way and then another.'

Board of Trade Review

Hobart Paper 49

Transport Policy: Co-ordination through Competition
G. J. PONSONBY

1969   Out of print: available on microfiche at £2·50

'... Mr Ponsonby has done us a substantial service in presenting this rigorous exposition of the economics of internal cross-subsidisation in transport. To have done more would have required a far longer book. . . . Such a longer book, when it comes, will owe a great debt to this paper for clearing the ground in a most lucid and systematic way. It is a welcome contribution to the literature on economic policy for the transport industry.'

Journal of Transport Economics & Policy